CU00692870

The Best Years of Our Lives?

Secondary Education in York 1900-1985

Van Wilson

Published by York Archaeological Trust 2010
47 Aldwark, York YO1 7BX
www.yorkarchaeology.co.uk

Designed and typeset by Gordon Webber
Cover design by Gordon Webber

Printed by
Zebra Print Management

ISBN No. 978-1 874454 49 6

Front cover: *Nunthorpe Art Room 1950 (Millthorpe School),*
Mill Mount Class 1930s (York City Archives)

Back cover: *School milk at break time 1950s (York City Archives),*
Cricket Team 1888 (Archbishop Holgate's School)

Contents

Foreword

York is a city which entwines itself round the heart for many reasons, its reputation for good schools among them. Some of my memories go back to the Second World War when, at eight years old or thereabouts, I stood in front of Poppleton Road Elementary School looking at the huge hole which had been made by a bomb, smartly severing it into two pieces. The sight of rubble and the smell of acrid smoke really brought home to me the reality of war.

My brother was a pupil at Archbishop Holgate's School when it was housed in that lovely building in Lord Mayor's Walk. Many years later I was invited back there when it had moved further out of the city. I saw St Peter's from the top of a number eight bus, from time to time, and always thought it looked like picture book illustrations of an Oxbridge college; when I was eventually asked there I thought it had retained its dignity very well. Both Bootham School and The Mount were, to me, slightly removed, and in a different orbit, and St Margaret's at Escrick in a different universe altogether.

The place which has had an abiding influence on me was York College for Girls, a church school which was made possible for me by winning something called the Brotherton Scholarship, enabling my parents to send me there. Our headmistress, Helena Randall, and all our teachers were remarkable women, bent on passing on their impeccable standards of behaviour to us: good manners, courtesy, thoughtfulness, so many of the values which don't appear to be important now. No eating in the street, no peeking over the playground wall at the Minster School choir boys, of course! Doing prep to the sound of the Minster bells; attending services and being confirmed there; walking to school through The Shambles; so many memories leaving imprints on the mind which only became consciously significant much later in my life and have never faded. I still meet with some of the friends I made there. We have even held Old Girls' dinners in the dining room, which has been turned into a restaurant since the school was closed.

And so to my years as the first woman Chancellor of York University, a very different world from the one I worked in, but tremendously fulfilling and satisfying; I believe that Helena Randall would have considered that to be my crowning moment since she regarded a life spent in education as paramount.

Many of the university staff are reluctant to leave York in retirement, which I understand very well. I left the city at the age of twenty to study music in London; but only physically: my heart and spirit are still there, with my parents and my brother Peter, who rest in Acomb churchyard.

Introduction

September 2010 marks the 25th anniversary of the reorganisation of secondary schools in York to comprehensives. Over the course of the 20th century, York saw huge changes in secondary education. After the Second World War, selection at the age of 11 took place, and by the early 1960s there were five grammar, 16 secondary modern and four independent schools. Today the independent schools remain but the rest have been replaced by nine comprehensive schools.

It is impossible in this publication to cover every school in York. I have chosen to include fifteen schools to represent the breadth and variety which existed in secondary education, with a combination of male and female voices. Although I would have loved to produce a history of each individual school, (and there is certainly enough material), space prohibits this, but I hope this book does give a flavour of what it was like to attend, and in some cases, to teach in, different types of York schools. I felt it was important also to avoid any kind of bias and to represent different viewpoints about such important milestones as the 11 plus selection system, and the varying individual experiences of how the system worked in practice.

Most, though not all, of the people whose stories are featured in these pages, look back on their school days fondly, and with a sense of pride. Although some were unhappy at school, even experiencing bullying, most of them did not want to dwell on the negative side of their school days.

Everyone has their own different memories of secondary school, happy, sad, serious or funny. Some of the stories in the book are very entertaining. It is not always the exam results that we remember, but who we sat next to, and how we were treated by the teachers. Many recall school as the place where deep friendships were cemented, which have lasted throughout life, though, for others, their closest friendships were formed later.

My own, like most people's, experiences of secondary school were mixed. I remember, at the age of 11, forming a secret society and meeting each lunchtime behind the gym, which was out of bounds. I recall cookery lessons where we produced rock cakes, stuffed tomatoes and cauliflower au gratin, as well as an 'invalid's breakfast', which even the dog refused to eat. My friend and I enjoyed writing Victorian melodramas at the age of 12, which four of us performed in front of our year. At 14, I was put off classical music, and Mozart in particular, (but thankfully not forever) by the music master who made us follow the score of Eine Kleine Nachtmusik. If I lost the place and started chatting, I was sent into the music store room to write out the words of an LP cover. The master had nicknames for every girl in the class. Two girls with blonde plaits were always addressed as 'stoat' and 'weasel'. I remember playing hockey in winter and freezing in an aertex shirt and shorts, whilst the games mistress ran around in tracksuit, scarf, hat and gloves and kept lovely and warm.

At 16, I was constantly being sent to the headmistress's office for being seen without my beret, and if we talked to boys at the gate behind the school, we would incur the wrath of the mistress on duty, who would be watching to see if any boy put a foot onto school property (as if they were alien beings). But I began to develop a love of history, writing essays in which I imagined I was Mary Queen of Scots or Sir Edmund Hillary conquering Everest, and I discovered Shakespeare and wonderful writers like Hardy and Lawrence, Jane Austen and the First World War poets.

No school is perfect, though most people agree that school life is better now than it was in the past. Hopefully there is more awareness of what a child needs. Most of the people I spoke to believe that education should equip young people for the future, and not just be a treadmill, a passive world of 'talk and chalk', a 'one size fits all' experience which pays no attention to individualism and creativity. But rather that it should unlock the future, giving young people the tools to manage what lies ahead. The profession of teaching is probably the most important job of all, carrying with it the responsibility for young people's development and progress. There are examples of how particular teachers inspired and encouraged children, and some people even spoke of being disappointed that their old teachers had not lived to see them achieve success in later life, perhaps, even decades later, still seeking their approval.

For many people the perfect school would combine academic subjects with practical expertise, preparing boys and girls for real life, learning how to run a home, cope with finances, cope with work and cope with relationships.

One lady sums up her feelings about school.

The exams were over and I walked out of school when others were still in lessons, feeling a huge sense of relief, and not immediately caring how well I had done. I was like a prisoner seeing the fresh air for the first time in years. The future opened up before me, with a sense of hope and possibility. Perhaps that is what school should do, help us to learn, sow the seeds which will later come to fruition, then send us out with hope, to flourish in adult life.

Acknowledgements

As always, there are many people whose contributions have been essential to the production of this book. From York Archaeological Trust, I would like to thank Chief Executive John Walker, and Director of Attractions, Sarah Maltby, for their support, photographer Mike Andrews for his scanning of numerous photographs, designer Gordon Webber for his layout and design of the publication, and, most importantly, Archivist and Editor Christine Kyriacou whose support and encouragement, as well as organising, help with research and painstaking proof-reading, have been invaluable.

I would like to thank the following organisations for their financial support of this project : Friends of York Archaeological Trust, Robert Kiln Charitable Trust, Sheldon Memorial Trust, Patricia and Donald Shepherd Trust, York Common Good Trust, the Yorkshire Architectural and York Archaeological Society, and Yorkshire Philosophical Society.

I am very grateful to Dame Janet Baker for her excellent foreword to the book. Grateful thanks go particularly to all those who shared stories (and sometimes photographs) from their schooldays, which I am sure will afford as much pleasure to the reader as they have to me:

Michael and Valerie Allen, Mary Barr, Thérèse Barton Rowan, Kathleen (Katie) Bonney, Joyce Botham, Darrell Buttery, Joan Campbell, Eileen Carter, Bernadette Cass, Maureen Chevens, Douglas Church, Glenn Cockerill, Joyce Cockerill, Mary Collier, Dorothy Cook, John Dale, Nancy Dawson, Anne Ellison, Godfrey Fowkes, Sheila Goater, David Gray, Neal Guppy, Colin Henderson, Ken Humphreys, Ian Johnson, Tim Kjeldsen, Jean Leeman, John Lightfoot, June Lloyd-Jones, Michael May, Vera McHugh, Brenda Milner, Richard Nihill, Heather Norton, Nicholas Page, Janet Pigott, Richard Potter, Mike Race, Joan Sadler, Michael Sargent, Edna Scott, Gillian Sowray, Ian Stead and Lynne Townend.

I wish to thank the following for help with queries –
Bernard Barr, Rosanne Bostock, Diane Church, Rupert Griffiths, John Langton, Philippa Pinder, David Poole, Ben Reeves, Erica Taylor, as well as David Main, local history librarian, and the staff of York City Archives, especially Joy Cann who always goes out of her way to assist.

Thanks are due to the following for the use of photographs –
Oliver Bostock, Christine Cockett, Jo Dodd, Marketing Manager of Bar Convent, Lynsey Fanning of the Northern Echo, Christine Kyriacou, Lauren Marshall and Jeremy Phillips of the Merchant Adventurers' Hall, Rob Maw, David Robinson, who copied the photos of Bootham, Sonia Murray-Kydd for photographs from 'Imagine York', also to York Oral History Society for use of material and photographs, and Mike Race for help with transport and copying photographs.

I would like to thank the following for access to their archives and, in some cases, giving us guided tours of their schools –
Bridget Morris, Bootham School Archivist; Sharon Lang, Business Manager of All Saints' School, (previously the home of Mill Mount Grammar School); John Harris, head teacher of Archbishop Holgate's, and Jacqui Sissons, PA to the head; Staff of La Vecchia Scuola restaurant (York College for Girls); and from Millthorpe School – Steve Smith, acting head (also head of Fulford School), Gareth Davies, deputy head, Paul Monteagle, library manager, Lesley Buckley, PA to the head, and Mike Doss, archivist.

I would like to dedicate this book to my three closest friends at school, Rosanne Lomax, Janis Winn, who sadly died a few years ago, and Heather Whyte, each of whom brought something to my life which enriched it. And to two teachers, Edith Horne and Marie Wood, who encouraged in me a love of language and literature.

Education for All

The history of education in England is inextricably linked with politics, and major changes are always introduced by the government of the time. The Elementary Education Act of 1870, under the Liberal government of Gladstone, was the first piece of legislation to deal specifically with education for children in Britain, when it brought in education for all and made school attendance compulsory for children aged five to eleven. Prior to this, those who could afford to give their children more than a very basic education (which amounted to the 'three Rs') sent them to private schools or employed tutors or governesses. Schools were run by the church or private individuals and some offered places for poorer children, due to the support of wealthy philanthropists.

Before the Education Act, York had a number of private schools, ranging from the illustrious St Peter's, founded in 627 AD, to small establishments in schoolmasters' homes where a dozen or so children might attend. The York Chronicle of May 1777 advertised Thomas Bramley's School in Pavement which offered

> *'writing, arithmetic, book-keeping, merchants' accounts, geometry, trigonometry, algebra, astronomy, tangents, secants, logarithms, mechanics and fluxions'.*

Private education for girls was much more refined, and limited, of course, and Mr Brown's establishment in York charged 14 guineas a year in 1779 for

> *'French, drawing, music and dancing'.*

After the Education Act, new elementary schools were built to accommodate the large numbers of children who would now be attending. They had large classes, usually between 40 and 50 children, and were often housed in inadequate buildings. They were undenominational and funded by the local council, which was a blow to the church schools. The 'School Board men' were appointed to ensure that children did attend. The 1891 Education Act made elementary education free for all but many children also had to work, as families relied on their wages, and some could only attend school in their 'spare time'.

The first York School Board in 1889 resulted in four new 'Board' schools being built, by the renowned York architect Walter Brierley, three of which still exist as schools today. The first (no longer a school) was Shipton Street, built in 1891, followed by Fishergate in 1893, Park Grove in 1895, and the fourth, known as Brierley's masterpiece, Scarcroft School which opened in 1896. These were also known as triple decker schools, with infants on the ground floor, juniors on the next one, and older children up to 14 in the top deck. Brierley also designed Acomb School on Front Street, Poppleton Road School and Haxby Road School.

In 1888 there were 14 Church of England schools, four nonconformist and three Roman Catholic schools in the city. By 1902 there were 15 church schools, (with 6914 pupils), one Wesleyan, (566 pupils), three

Catholic (1270 pupils) and five board schools (4819 pupils). At the end of the 19th century, the street directories list 65 small private schools in the city, including Mrs Armstrong's at Fulford Field House, Mr Barnes on the Mount, the Misses Croft's School in Petergate, and the Misses Camidge's establishment in Monkgate.

Scarcroft School (Van Wilson)

The Education Act of 1902, called the Balfour Act after Arthur Balfour, the new Conservative prime minister, led to the introduction of secondary schools, either higher grade or fee-paying. School boards were abolished and the importance of private schools diminished. The York Education Committee was set up in September 1903 and a new act by the Liberal government in 1907 meant that each private school which received a grant, had to offer a number of free places (scholarships) to pupils from elementary schools.

Over the coming years, the York Education Service brought in a health service, child guidance clinic, schools for special needs including an open air school for delicate children, school meals, a youth service and careers advice.

Scarcroft School class with teacher Miss Evans 1908 (York Oral History Society)

However there was still a wide gap between the children who attended elementary schools to the age of 14, and those who undertook more advanced education. Queen Anne's School was initially housed at the Brook Street Pupil Teachers' Centre, providing secondary education for those who wished to go into teaching. In 1910, the school moved to a new building in Queen Anne's Road, Bootham, the first to be built by the York authority exclusively for secondary education. Changes in education slowed down during the First World War but in 1918, the school leaving age was raised to fourteen. 80 per cent of children received no formal education after fourteen but for those who did, the School Certificate was introduced for 16 year olds, which was made up of examinations in nine subjects. To obtain the qualification, all the subjects had to be passed. Successful pupils could go on to take the Higher School Certificate at the age of 18, as preparation for university. In 1919 St Peter's School agreed to give five places to scholarship boys each year and in 1920 two more secondary schools opened in the city, Mill Mount for girls, and Nunthorpe for boys.

SAMPLE QUESTIONS FROM 1933 PAPER
FOR ADMISSION TO SECONDARY EDUCATION

1. **Complete the following with a suitable word –**

   A bale of....
   A keg of....
   A hank of...
   A swarm of...
   A quire of...
   A brace of...
   A litter of...
   A horde of...
   A brood of...
   A shoal of...

2. **What do we call a room which**

   Has a lot of books in it
   Is at the top of the house just under the roof
   Is used for washing plates and dishes
   Is used for storing food
   Is where clerks and typists work

3. **Explain why the following are wrong or absurd**

   The following notice appeared in a shop window. "If you cannot read this notice, please inquire at the house next door".

   The discovery of America by Columbus in 1492 was an outstanding event in the 14th century.

   He ordered his servant to return at once by telegram.

After partaking of a hearty breakfast, the balloon started off.

He watched the mouse running away from the cat with a smile on his face.

With set purpose he accidentally shot the burglar.

The ewe in the churchyard is nearly 300 years old.

4. Put down the missing number (examples are given of this)

17, 21, 29, 33,

55, 47, 39, 31,

1, 3, 9, 27,

½, ¼, ⅛,

5. Write an essay on one of the following

The four seasons

The posters at a railway station

A circus you have seen

The wonders of wireless

The adventures of a damaged shilling which no shopkeeper will accept

The Hadow Report of 1926 recommended a break in schooling at 11, when pupils would have to be transferred to a separate secondary school. But it was the 1944 Education Act, devised by the Conservative 'President of the Board of Education', Richard 'Rab' Butler, which brought in the new tripartite system and abolished tuition fees in secondary schools. Elementary schools became junior schools and an examination at the age of 11, the 11 plus, consisting of papers in verbal and non-verbal reasoning, followed by maths and English, was used to select pupils for either grammar, secondary modern or technical schools. In practice, technical schools often became vehicles for further education or day release after 15 and pupils transferred, at the age of 11, to either grammar school or secondary modern.

The new act was seen as a positive thing by many, as it guaranteed free secondary education and opened the door for children from poorer families to take advantage of this. But others felt it was ludicrous to determine a child's secondary education and potentially their future career on the basis of what 'amounted to an IQ test'. In theory, dividing children according to their ability, so that they would benefit most from their secondary education, might be a good thing, but in practice it became a question of passing or failing, and therefore the secondary modern schools were perceived as second-best. Additionally, certain primary schools 'coached' pupils by setting practice papers on a weekly or monthly basis in examination conditions, whereas some children taking the 11 plus had never seen a sample paper before, which seemed grossly unfair to many.

The 11 plus was a crucial time in a child's life. Many talk of how they were desperate to pass, for their parent's sake as much as their own. As a result of the exam, only 20 per cent of children were given places at grammar school, and 80 per cent of children went to secondary modern schools, with the option of further education at technical college.

In 1947, the school leaving age was again raised, this time to 15. George Tomlinson, the Minister for Education from 1947 to 1951, came to speak in York and told the story of a girl who, after her first day at secondary school, was asked by her father, "Well have they educated you then?", to which she replied, "No I've got to go again tomorrow". The General Certificate of Education came in, at both Ordinary and Advanced Level, in 1951. Unlike the

---

LATIN (2).
(GRAMMAR, SYNTAX, AND SET BOOKS.)
Tuesday,
July 11th, 1933.
2—4.

UNIVERSITIES OF MANCHESTER, LIVERPOOL, LEEDS, SHEFFIELD, AND BIRMINGHAM.

———

SCHOOL CERTIFICATE AND
MATRICULATION EXAMINATIONS.

———

TWO HOURS.

Begin each question on a fresh page.

Candidates must answer both Section A and Section B.

Section A.

A 1. Give the ablative singular of *neuter exercitus, vir integer, breve tempus*, and the genitive plural of *ingens classis, tristior pater, nullum iter*

A 2. Give the Latin for *such things, bravely, on the bridge, thirty women, that city of yours, a greater war*

A 3. Parse giving the principal parts. *expellis, protectas, recipi, consentiant, manerem.*

A 4. Give in Latin the actual words of Caesar (*Oratio Recta*) from *si to redeant* in the following passage Caesar Germanis respondet, si obsides ab illis dentur, sese pacem esse facturum, domum statim redeant.

Latin paper 1933 (Godfrey Fowkes)

School Certificate, examinations were taken in individual subjects and were marked separately.

As early as 1957, the York Education Committee asked the Chief Education Officer to prepare plans with a view to eventual abolition of 11 plus selection. But the proposals were too far-reaching. In 1965, the CSE or Certificate in Secondary Education was introduced in secondary modern schools. The level was lower than the GCE but a CSE at grade one would equal a C pass in the GCE. In July of that year, the Department of Education (under Harold Wilson's Labour government) sent out a circular stating that the government's objective was to end selection by 11 plus and asking authorities to submit proposals for a comprehensive education. York's local authority formed a Development Plan in 1968, advocating a middle school system, with schools for 5-9 year olds, 9-13 year olds and 13-16 or 18 year olds. This was approved in principle but it never happened.

In 1970, the new Conservative government, under Edward Heath, stated that local authorities were not compelled to move to comprehensive education. The school leaving age was raised to 16 in 1973, but it would be another 12 years before the tripartite system was abolished in York. The 1970s proved to be a something of a yo-yo in terms of its education policies. In 1974, the new Labour government reaffirmed the decision to proceed with a move to comprehensives. The 1976 Education Act asked local authorities to plan for non-selective systems of education. This was repealed by the Conservatives in 1979. It must have been very difficult and confusing for Education Committees at this time! Another factor complicating matters was the change of local authority from York to North Yorkshire County Council, which changed the boundaries of the city and caused more administrative upheaval.

But the ball had started rolling, and most authorities in England had already changed to comprehensive education by 1975. Schools were inevitably becoming larger, as due to the post-war baby boom, numbers of pupils rose from 175,000 in 1946 to 448,000 in 1977. The Education Act of 1980 introduced funding for more assisted places in private schools, and gave parents more choice and more power on governing bodies of schools.

In 1985, comprehensive education finally arrived in York. The Education Reform Act of 1988 established the National Curriculum and unified teaching throughout the country, giving parents a choice of secondary schools, though it was largely determined by catchment area. The new system of GCSEs (General Certificate in Secondary Education) to replace GCEs and CSEs, began to be taught in 1986, and after two years of the syllabus, the first actual exams were taken in 1988.

In more recent years comprehensive schools have been encouraged to specialise in certain subjects and focus on excellence in those areas.

1939 Arithmetical Table Book, W.T.Owbridge, Hull
(Christine Kyriacou)

CHAPTER 2

Higher Grade Schools

Before the Second World War, York had eight higher grade schools: Knavesmire, Manor, the Model School, Shipton Street, Priory Street, Castlegate, St George's and St Wilfrid's, the last two being Catholic schools.

Shipton Street Higher Grade, which had been the first of the board schools in 1891, taught English composition and grammar, literature, French, history, geography, arithmetic, geometry, chemistry, art, housecraft (cookery, laundry, housewifery), needlework, religious instruction, PE and games. In 1910 there were 228 boys, 278 in the girls' department and 202 infants. The boys department closed in 1912 and eventually moved to Park Grove. In 1942, the senior girls transferred to the new Water Lane (later Burton Stone Lane) School and Shipton Street became a junior school.

Shipton Street School Report 1937 (Van Wilson)

Priory Street School had been built in 1858 next door to Wesley Chapel, (now the Rock Church), as a Wesleyan Methodist School. By 1870 it had accommodation for 600 and a teacher's residence at the side. A 'select class' received tuition in algebra, Euclid, mensuration, book-keeping, composition, land surveying, advanced drawing and ornamental penmanship. In 1905 the school was extended with a new building in front of the west wing. It had a good reputation and a number of children came in from outside the city by train, including Eliza Kirby who was born in 1891.

We came in from Tollerton and one of the oldest boys or oldest girls was allowed to go at playtime and put the gas oven on low. If your mother sent you with a meat pie, they could put it in the oven and it was nice and warm by twelve o'clock.

I remember being whacked on the hand. The teacher lost her temper and got cross with me, and instead of using the cane, used a little pointer. I yelled terribly and the headmistress came downstairs to see what was wrong. I hated school, the only thing I liked was the first half hour, the Scripture lesson, and I liked needlework, Monday and Tuesday afternoons. I won a first prize three years in succession, and it was a special prize the last year for neat sewing.

Priory Street 1900. Wesley Chapel on left, the school on left behind trees. (York Oral History Society)

[Eliza was prone to occasionally fainting]. *And when I'd faint at school, I informed them, "My mother always gives me a little brandy", but they gave me sal volatile.*Ella Beswick was born in 1906 and also attended Priory Street.

I was not a brilliant scholar but received a good education. I always wanted to be a nurse, but the poor subject I had was needlework. In this class I was rather ridiculed, and this was a great disadvantage, because I couldn't stand correction from the teacher. We never received any corporal punishment, it was enough for me to be sent to Mr Skerry, because I would stand outside his door in floods of tears. Our assistant headmaster, Mr Ellis, was not so kind. He could make you feel foolish. Our sports teacher, Mr Turner, was a very good man and from him I learnt discipline in sport. I remember being given 'out' at rounders in a match and I knew I wasn't. I was going to say something to the umpire and I got one look from Mr Turner and handed in my bat. The next day it was explained to me that you never argue with the referee or umpire. Pity it doesn't still happen today.

I left home at quarter to eight to get the train to York, and didn't get home until quarter to six. But we were allowed to stay in the classrooms and we did our homework. Or perhaps we would be allowed a game of rounders. Our great delight was when we went to the station, we could run through the bar walls at Micklegate. I once missed the train and the station master took me into the Station Hotel and gave me some tea and hot buttered teacake. We used to take a packed lunch but if it was a day with domestic science, we were allowed to eat what we had made. Occasionally mother ran out of bread and I used to go down to Boyes's and have a wonderful dinner. I remember their sponge puddings which were delicious. Or I could go to the top of Priory Street where there was a lovely baker's shop.

The washing facilities at school could leave much to be desired. You could wash your hands and I remember Miss Greenwood saying to one of the girls, "Here, take the key, [to the washroom], your neck needs a wash". But that girl's mother had been a war widow from the First World War, and there were no pensions, she used to take in lodgers. So there was very little time for her between looking after the lodgers and themselves.

At the end of term we had a concert when we were all expected to do something. I remember with my friend Elsie Absome, deciding that we would sing 'Underneath the Gaslight Glitters'. We put our heart and soul into it, but were so pathetic that we were told never to sing again, and that I should stick to recitation which evidently was one of my good points.

Priory Street Class 1920s (York Oral History Society)

Hewson Thorpe went to Priory Street School in the 1920s.

We had to pay in those days, I think it was seven and sixpence. One of the teachers, Miss Shepherd, she was 90 when she died. We called her 'Pretty Polly', she was a real fancy dresser, a proper little china doll. We had an excellent headmaster, Mr Skerry. He used to cycle up Priory Street on one of these sit-up-and-beg bikes, and woe betide anybody who hadn't got a cap on. You had to go to his room! Or if he saw you skylarking about, you were 'for it'. When he retired, his deputy took over, Mr Ellis, and he was a holy terror, scared the daylights out of everybody. The whole tone of the school seemed to go down. When we got to Standard 6, we were split into two streams. You either took a general course or a commercial course. I didn't like woodwork or chemistry so I took the commercial course. I got certificates for shorthand, book-keeping, typewriting and arithmetic.

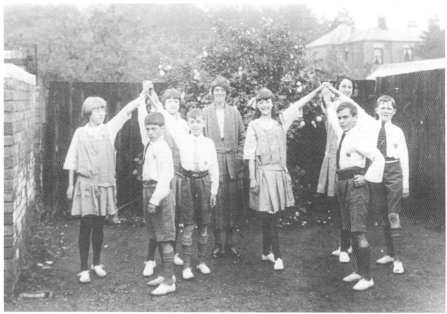

Dancing at Priory Street School 1910 (York Oral History Society)

Joan Sadler attended from 1933 to 1936.

It was mixed but no mixed classes. There was a girls' entrance and a boys' entrance.

I remember the netball post was the square piece that's still there. The headmaster lived on site. He was mad on algebra, but the figures and lines didn't mean anything to me. I often wondered what good they would be. But he was keen on spelling and handwriting. I think most of us left to be very good spellers. Miss Petty was the cookery teacher. *She was a staunch Methodist and very keen. I can remember swimming lessons, and life-saving classes at St. George's baths. I got two certificates for life-saving, my sister and I belonged to York City Swimming Club at the time.*

I can remember netball and hockey. The boys did football. Two of the boys, Terry Walker and Gordon Winters, played for a Yorkshire team which was quite something in those days.

I can't remember any science. For cookery, you prepared them the night before. We made nothing exotic, everything was very basic, scones and buns, and how to make sandwiches properly. I thought how strict the headmaster was, Mr Ellis, I never liked him, I guess because of the algebra. When he used to come round, if you were writing, the pencil had to point over your right shoulder, and it still

Rowntrees' Keep Fit Class 1930s (York Oral History Society)

*does. We couldn't write with a pen until we moved into the upstairs
school. I was lucky to have good handwriting, I loved composition
and writing, and I still do. There's never a day when I don't write a
letter to somebody, and my desk lid is never closed.*

Joan left school to work at Rowntree's but her education did not come to
an end.

*We went to day school there, English one half day a week and keep
fit another half day. Then we went back some evenings to do more
keep fit. I've always been involved in the young people's theatre there.
I started in 1936, the Rowntree's theatre was built in 1935, so it's
always been part of my life.*

Rowntree's began to offer part-time classes to its factory boys and girls in
the first decade of the century. Some other York firms followed suit, such
as Cooke, Troughton and Sims and the GPO. The policy of day release
classes for apprentices and other workers ensured that education could
continue.

Priory Street School closed in 1948. In the 1970s it became a Sports and
Community Centre, and today
is the home of York Council for
Voluntary Service and a conference
centre, offering video and wireless
telephone conferencing facilities,
interactive digital whiteboards,
wi-fi internet connection, solar
powered mobile phone recharging
facilities, i-phone projectors, high
resolution data-projectors and
laptops, and a portable IT training
suite with 12 workstations. A far
cry from the higher grade school it
once housed!

Priory Street Centre 2010 (Christine Kyriacou)

– CHAPTER 3 –

Grammar Schools For Boys

Samuel Johnson defined a grammar school as 'a school in which the learned languages [Latin and Greek] are classically taught' and this was historically the case. But the Grammar Schools Act of 1840 made it legal to use a school's income to cover many other subjects in the curriculum. Eventually two types of grammar school existed, maintained grammar schools, funded by the state, and direct grant ones which combined state funding with private fees.

Once the tripartite system came into being in 1944, there were three grammar schools for girls in York, but only two for boys, Nunthorpe and Archbishop Holgate's. Both had begun as secondary schools.

ARCHBISHOP HOLGATE'S GRAMMAR SCHOOL

Cricket Team 1888 (*Archbishop Holgate's School*)

Archbishop Holgate's, the second oldest boys' school in York, after St Peter's, was founded by Archbishop Robert Holgate in 1546, with money obtained from the Dissolution of the Monasteries. He was the first archbishop to take the oath accepting the Royal Supremacy (under Henry VIII) and renouncing the authority of Rome. For the first 300 years the school was located in Ogleforth. It fell on hard times, and for some years did little more than educate the Minster choir boys, but in the 19th century its fortunes were revived and it became highly successful, largely under the headship of Robert Daniel (1846 to 1882).

The school moved to Lord Mayor's Walk in 1858 merging with the Yeoman School which had been a practising school for St John's Teacher Training College there. Discipline was very strict and school hours were long with short holidays. In 1860 there were 18 day boys and 60 boarders. The list of requirements for the latter included 2 suits, 6 day shirts, 3 night shirts, 3 night caps, 6 pairs of stockings, 4 pairs of drawers, 4 under waistcoats, 3 black or 6 coloured silk neckerchiefs, 6 pocket handkerchiefs, 3 pairs of shoes, 1 pair of slippers, 2 hats or one hat and one cap, one hairbrush and comb, one tooth comb and brush, one clothes brush, one great coat, one umbrella, Bible and prayer book.

Archbishop Holgate's Grammar School c1910 (Archbishop Holgate's School)

By 1899 there were 140 boys at the school and extensions were built in 1904 and 1913. The fees were £7 10s. The curriculum was also changing, and subjects comprised Latin, physics and chemistry, geography, history, English grammar, composition and literature, mathematics, drawing, technical subjects, and religious instruction. A modern language, and vocal music and drill, which had been extras, were now included. The Quadringenary Magazine celebrating the school's 400th birthday, quotes how in 1895, 'On Sundays, the boarders, dressed in Eton suits and either silk hats or mortar boards, went to the Minster or for a time to St Michael le Belfrey. They sat in box seats'.

During the First World War, the school suffered severely from frequent changes in staff. 70 masters and old boys joined the army. The headmaster, William Johnson, resigned to become an Anglican minister. The new head was Percy Vintner, and his two sisters, Jenny and Fanny, graduates from Cambridge and Dublin, came in to replace male teachers. Part of the school playing fields was used as allotments, with boys undertaking the cultivation and selling the produce. In 1915 the school Cadet Corps was officially recognised by the War Office, and affiliated to the 5th Battalion Prince of Wales's Own, West Yorkshire Regiment. During the war, boys from the school received the Military Cross, CMG, and Military Medal, and the French master M Duchene, was awarded the Croix de Guerre with three bars. 46 boys and masters were killed on active service and a memorial service was held at St Maurice's Church in 1919.

The Mitre Cover 1918 (Archbishop Holgate's School)

The Old Boys' Society was formed in 1919. The members met regularly and in early 1920 held an 'Old Boys' Smoker' at the Windmill Hotel, with recitations and monologues and 'very fine songs rendered by Messrs Bellerby, Cundall, Hartley, Kilvington, Welburn and Lakeman'. In 1923 the school memorial library was dedicated, in memory of the boys and masters lost during the war. Extra sports on offer included football, cricket, shooting, swimming, athletics and Swedish drill.

Football Team 1935, with headmaster Percy Vintner in centre.
Raymond Connell far right on front row. (York Oral History Society)

In 1937 Mr Vintner was succeeded by Arthur Hodgson. With the advent of another war in 1939, after-school activities were curtailed because of the blackout, although it was only the boarders who spent nights in the school air raid shelters. During the summer it was possible to pursue activities such as natural history, boating, cycling, angling, hockey, painting, geology, table tennis, and the more sedate matchbox collecting, philosophy, radio, philately, Hornby model railways and Sunday armchair musical evenings. Boys and masters had to take turns in fire watching, and patrolling the buildings and dormitories. The Air Training Corps, which was connected with RAF Linton on Ouse, took part in aircraft spotting. The school records that over a thousand old boys served their country. In 1951 a memorial to the 61 who had lost their lives, was unveiled.

Archbishop Holgate's School Air Defence Corps 116 Squadron 1940 (Archbishop Holgate's School)

In 1943, York Education Committee allowed the school to purchase the Brook Street Centre (which had become Queen Anne's School until it moved to Queen Anne's Road), as an extension, at a cost of £5068. The governors wished the school to be independent, and wanted to increase the fees to £42 p.a. but there was opposition to this and in 1949 the school became a controlled voluntary aided secondary grammar school, although it still retained something of the ethos of a public school. By 1955, numbers had increased to 520.

During that decade, dance classes with the girls from Queen Anne's School began again, and prefects started to wear gowns. School visits to Germany to promote Anglo-German relations were undertaken. Hiking, badminton, basketball and soccer were added to the list of extra curricular sports.

Neal Guppy joined the school in 1949. His favourite subjects were

chemistry and physics. One of the teachers was Mr Holderness.

We used to call him Nero because he fiddled. He'd written a few chemistry books and we used them as the base of our learning. He appeared to be very cynical and down to earth but he had a harsh sense of humour. He would pick on us individually at different times but we didn't hold it against him because it was more like a theatrical act. He'd start off, "I've been teaching for many, many years, but never in my life have I seen so many absurd answers to questions. This class has reached a record low level". He had wonderful tales about people who came to a sticky end. He was invited to America by the Dupont Chemical Company. Niagara Falls was one of the places he went to. He said, "The Falls cascade over the top and just above that was a bridge and it was a common spot for people to commit suicide. While I was there, three people attempted it, and one got stuck on an island". Eventually up goes the hand, "What happened?" "He fell over, three hours afterwards"!! He also went to the American Dolomites where suddenly a geyser would erupt, he told us with great relish. "We stayed in a hotel there". So up goes my hand, "No geysers came up over the hotel then, sir?" He just looked over the top of his glasses, "No, Guppy, I'm sure that is a great disappointment to you".

Neal recalls experiments in the lab.

When you produce chlorine, it's a heavier gas than air, and if you're near a sink, it'll drop in. It was O'Driscoll, a boy in my class, who'd forgotten this, and with a lighted splint going past, set fire to the sink. He also smashed a large glass flask. Up went the eyebrows from Nero and then some sarcastic comment. Later on he smashed a Liebitz condenser, much more expensive piece of equipment. So rather wearily, Nero said, "What are you hoping to do?" "To become a surgeon". "Oh really? Well if you succeed, O'Driscoll, will you please contact me? I'll make sure I don't live within fifty miles of you". And O'Driscoll became a successful surgeon!

Holderness had a tale about one lad. Phosphorous is kept in oil and looks like sticks of yellow chalk and this lad decided to pinch one,

Chemistry Master Albert Holderness, second from right, and John Lambert with 500,000th copy of their chemistry book 1962
(Archbishop Holgate's School)

put it in his back pocket and walked home and it just took fire. He told us about this poor lad burning his backside. And he was full of these stories, which of course really appealed to us.

In the sixth year, I decided to leave to take up aero engineering. And whenever I misbehaved, it was 'Aviator Guppy', sarcastically. But as I was leaving, he stopped and very warmly shook hands and wished me the best of luck so he was quite warm and thoughtful.

Albert Holderness was one of the few men to have been both pupil and master at the school, captain of the school in 1920, and editor of the magazine, the Mitre. The Yorkshire Evening Press reported in April 1958 that the School Certificate Chemistry Book (published in 1936) by joint authors Albert Holderness and John Lambert (another old boy) had sold its 500,000th copy. Holderness retired in 1963 and died in 1968.

Neal recalls other characters.

Ken Parsons was the art teacher, who had very little control of his class but was an earnest artist and gave me the vision to understand how to look at a work of art, how to look at the world from quite another angle. George Robinson was perhaps my favourite teacher. He was maths and physics, and he was excellent. When he was doing blackboard work, if he made an error, and somebody pointed it out, he would immediately praise the person, correct himself and carry on. And that is the sign of a good teacher.

Lulu Mayes was our music teacher. He taught us not to sing the words of a song but the melody first. He'd have a stick which he would tap on the bench, and would go, 'Lu, lu, lu, lu, lu, lu", and we'd try and get him excited, and he would say, "Shut up, shut up", get very excited and the stick would break in two. Then a loud cheer. But he recognised that by the time we got to the third year, there were half a dozen of us interested in orchestral music. He had a hi-fi, so he'd send us off to his study to listen to music. That's how I first learned to enjoy Ravel's 'Daphne and Chloe' suite and things like Richard Strauss, that were new to us.

Neal Guppy in music class, third from left on second row 1953 (Neal Guppy)

Neal started a model aircraft club at the school.

I designed a glider for them to make and set it up in the physics lab. We'd got a teacher voluntarily helping, prepared to stay on and see we behaved ourselves.

Neal Guppy with his model glider 1955
(*Neal Guppy*)

They thought football wasn't a game for gentlemen. I had to play rugby which I wasn't enthusiastic about. But the slightest bang and my nose would bleed. I was put into the house team because I ran faster than most people. I would run like hell and score a try, but more out of fear of a nosebleed!

Arthur Hodgson was headmaster until 1959. He died in 1961 at the age of 62. His obituary said that he was responsible for changing the school to the Rugby Union code, as 'he wanted to ensure his school would produce public-spirited type of boys'.

After the war, there was an intensive 13 month teacher training course, with experienced tutors, for those who had served in the war and wanted to teach.

There were hang over teachers but there were newer ones, many of them had been fighting in the war. They were people with life experience, not cushioned by being academic.

One of the great characters was the biology teacher, Buggie Allen, [Charles Allen]. *He would pick on certain students who didn't want to be in the classroom. "Do you realise that a third of our life is spent working? And you're going to be the kind of bloke who will be looking at the clock all the time and going home as soon as you can, and you'll be wasting a third of your life". It made me realise that if we're going to spend a great portion of our life doing something, we might as well be doing what we want to do. Buggie Allen was quite an important man in the Philosophical Society. There's a tree* [in the Museum Gardens] *with his name to it.*

There was a maths teacher who spat when he said things. We wrote in ink, most people used water soluble ink because you could get it off your clothes. But permanent ink stayed. I used to sit on the front row and my maths book was covered in splashes, so I had to use permanent ink otherwise the formulas would disappear before my eyes. But he knew all about architecture and ancient churches, and if we were doing maths, all we had to do was to say, "Sir, what's a machicolation?" He would then go on to describe it, and we could keep him going for 20 minutes, could sidetrack him very happily.

Archbishop Holgate's stuck to the traditions of Greek and Latin. After the war, the sciences were trying to progress and the classics people [were left behind]. I was disappointed because Archbishop Holgate's seemed to be looking backwards, and was sitting on its laurels, and reputation of the past. There was this old public school spirit which permeated the school, which belonged to Edwardian times. I would imagine that at Nunthorpe, the technology was taking a greater part and they would have better workshops. But we had some wonderful teachers. I think when Mr Frith came [in 1959], things changed very much.

I'd had six months of training at Bristol Aircraft Company but in the long run I ended up becoming a teacher. When I looked for a second career, I thought of George Robinson, if I could do half as well as he did and be as enthusiastic and carry that enthusiasm to the class, then it was a job worth doing.

(See Chapter 6 about Neal's time as a teacher at Derwent School).

The 1960s was a productive decade. There were many drama and musical productions, the choir was very active, there was barn dancing and jiving and a thriving school scout troop. In 1961, the school put on a revue entitled 'Let's Go Gay'! In 1962, Archbishop Holgate's entered the schools' television quiz show 'Top of the Form', but the team was beaten in the final round. In 1964 when Harold Wilson became the new Labour prime minister, the school held a Mock Election where the Conservatives were triumphant with 134 votes, with Labour a close second with 127. One boy, Harold Stuteley, won 14 votes for the 'National Association of Small Shopkeepers' party'. A school balloon debate took place, with boys taking the roles of Cassius Clay, Dr Who, Sir Alec Douglas-Home and Brigitte Bardot. The Mitre reported that 'this being a boys' school, I have no need to mention the winner's name'.

Staff and headmaster Donald Frith 1962 (Archbishop Holgate's School)

The new chapel in the boarding house was dedicated in summer 1967. By this time the school had a captain, vice captain, five house captains (for Boarders, Dean, Ebor, Holgate and Johnson), five prefects and 25 monitors.

Michael May joined Archbishop Holgate's in 1958 and was in Ebor house.

There was a sense of it being educationally a better school. I thought the 11 plus was a reasonable test of a child's abilities and it did sort out children into groups to show where they needed better education. I was always reasonable at things apart from science. English language has probably served me best over the years. I think they were looking to give you an all round education.

It was an old school with old facilities. Donald Frith was the head. I remember the French teacher, Milligan, (we called him Spike), used to pull you up by your sideburns or would throw the board eraser, that could give you quite a crack. Some of them were strict disciplinarians. There were a load of us taken down to the changing room and they gave us a couple of whacks with the slipper. One guy used to cane your hands. I don't think we looked upon it as being a breach of our human rights at that stage. I remember Mr Holderness. He had a saying if he ever saw somebody with a scouts badge. "Be prepared is your motto. Yes, be prepared to do no work". He was always sarcastic about the scouts.

Class at Archbishop Holgate's, Michael May, far right on second row, Les Bingham (Barbican Bookshop, York) far right on front row. c1959 (Michael May)

There was a teacher we called Bod who was small, round and bald headed with glasses. He had long shorts down to his knees. I remember him taking us for rugby and we had a scrum. He went into the middle to lecture to the front row and everybody collapsed on him. I got involved in sport, played rugby and cricket and did represent the school in inter-school competitions. I was a sprinter and faster than a lot of the kids that were older than me.

In 1959, Michael came first in the under 12s 100 yards and hurdles, second in long jump, and first in the 880 yards, winning the Junior Championship Cup. In 1960, he was in the house junior cricket team and in their winning match against Boarders, he and another boy were described as the 'demon bowlers'. In 1963, he was first in the intermediate 100 yards, 220 yards, 440 yards and long jump and won the intermediate individual championship cup.

My view is that schools now are too big and have to cater for too much. You've got such a big range of abilities. Although in some areas there are schools above comprehensives, there are no schools below them. Everyone has to mix and learn on the same level, it's too unwieldy. And you have teachers having to cope with teaching under duress. At Archbishop Holgate's, there was more discipline, less pupil moans, more interest in what you were doing from the class as a whole.

There wasn't the level of external happenings that there is now. You didn't have the internet and computer games, and you didn't know too much about what was going on around the world. You were more cocooned in your own environment, we made our own entertainment. We had more freedom because there wasn't the unpleasantness in the environment that there is now. You were allowed to grow up at your own pace.

In the summer of 1963 the school moved to its present site on Hull Road. Some boys who had time on their hands volunteered to help move books and equipment to the new site. They speak of being delighted by the feeling of light and space, as the school was set on top of a hill with fields surrounding it.

Archbishop Holgate's was the only state school in York to still have boarders. Richard Potter joined the school in 1967 but when his parents left York in 1971, he became a boarder and automatically went into Boarders house, though he had previously been in Holgate. The boarding house closed in the 1980s.

There were 50 boarders from 11 to 18 so I was in the middle. It was a bit of a shock at first as I went out at night as a day boy and we were sometimes drinking under age, all that stopped when we had to be in bed by 9pm. I have many memories of the boarding house, mostly good ones. We could use the school gym and pool and playing fields whenever we wanted. Every year there was a house rugby competition and the other houses had about 250 kids each so we always had to have kids from lower years in the team to make up numbers. One year we went all the way and won the school senior house rugby cup and we all played well as a team. I scored a try against my old house Holgate (my Dad's old house) which was very pleasing.

There was a bathroom in the boarding house which had five baths in it and we kept all the taps on full so all five filled up and overflowed. The bathroom had a 'step over' doorway like a ship, so water never leaked out. It had good drains, so we let the water flow over the baths and then either had water fights with hands under the tap, to direct a jet of water, or soap the passage floor between the baths so you could slide down the length of the room on your backside. This would all go well until water started to drip through the ceiling to the library below and then trouble…

We had to go every Sunday to Heslington church, usually to the 8am service as there were no hymns and it was shorter. One week we had to go to the 10am service as the service was filmed on 'Songs of Praise' that week. We did our usual thing and went on the back row and sang our own funny words to the hymns, thinking we couldn't be seen. When we got back we watched the delayed broadcast and saw the camera pan onto all the naughty boys in the back row laughing during the serious service.

Despite these episodes, Richard's future career went well and after studying at Nottingham, he became a lawyer in London, and is now a barrister in Sydney.

Nicholas Page started at Archbishop Holgate's in 1975.

It had a good name in York, a certain 'cachet' that perhaps Nunthorpe didn't have. My first couple of years were a bit unsettled but I was happy after that. I'm sure a lot of bullying did go on there. Music was very important for me. I was in the choir all the way up, I played the organ for the school carol service and Founder's Day. Speech days tended to have musical performances in them. I was in 'The Importance of Being Earnest', and 'The Sorcerer', Gilbert and Sullivan, and in the York Festival in 1982, I was in 'Paul Bunyan' at the Rowntree's Theatre [a joint production with Queen Anne's School].

Nicholas Page *(Christine Cockett)*

It seems that a pupil's enjoyment of a subject, often depended on the teacher.

We had a very good English teacher for the first two years who was able to communicate his subject enthusiastically. But then for O level we got a newly qualified teacher who wasn't very good and that dissuaded me from taking it further. Steve White, the history teacher, inspired me in many ways, not just in an interest in Tudor and Stuart history. He's a Catholic, and I've always been interested in church history. Robert Bunting and Barry Russell, and some of the other teachers were very encouraging about the music. We had a biology teacher called Mr Carner who was a very strict disciplinarian, I forget what it was we'd done as a class but he had a meter rule and by the end of the lesson, it had broken and there were only a few centimetres left. Corporal punishment only went in about 1980.

A lot of staff had retired and quite a few people came in the '60s and they had a less distant view of the boys than their predecessors. By that time the teachers didn't wear gowns except on very special occasions. There wasn't the formality that there had been. A new head, Michael Frost, came in 1978. The school hymn that had been sung with great gusto at the end of term and at Founder's Day for many years, was phased out. He taught French and was a very good teacher. The staff respected what he was doing on the whole. There were certainly some unruly boys. I think even at that age, you could sense there was a thin line between absolute chaos and order. Certainly Michael Frost was much more stern than Donald Frith. He knew how to restore order.

He was brought in, it seemed, to pave the way for comprehensive reorganisation. Everyone thought it was going to happen, sooner than it did. It was quite a live subject politically in York. Some of the staff who had strong feelings either one way or the other, made them known from time to time. I suspect there were more against it than for it, because as comprehensive education had been introduced in other parts of the country, people who wanted to teach in a grammar school, perhaps found their way into schools like Archbishop's.

By the time I got into the fifth form, the school was showing signs that it was unsustainable in the form that it was in. The range of subjects that it aspired to teach, were beginning to struggle, like the classics. At A level I did history, music and French. In French there were three of us, and in music there was just me. Whereas up to O level, teachers had to teach to the syllabus, in an A level class they could indulge their interests and passions more freely, so you were able to explore different things in a less structured way. We also did general studies, there was a cookery option and we'd go to Derwent School and use their kitchens. And I helped Burnholme out with a concert they were putting on. We'd had this feeling that anywhere else would be absolutely awful and when we actually got in there, it wasn't. It was certainly different at Archbishop's but whether it was actually superior, I'm not sure.

Since the school became comprehensive, obviously over the first few years there were problems that showed. Things settled down and it's altered a great deal. In many ways I'm jealous that I didn't have the opportunities that the pupils have there now.

A mixed school would have made life easier, all boys' schools have a particular character and ethos. I sometimes wish I'd had the chance to go to an independent school. I'd had this vision of ivy clad buildings and a chapel with stained glass and things like that, rather than 1950s concrete.

Many people feel they would like to go back to their schooldays, yet with the wisdom and experience of age. Perhaps George Bernard Shaw was right when he said, 'Youth is wasted on the young'. As Nicholas says,

If I'd had the insights that I have now and could have started school with them, I think I would have got more out of it.

Archbishop Holgate's became a mixed comprehensive school in 1985, and lost its sixth form, but in 2009 a new £4 million Learning Centre, funded by the Learning and Skills Council, and containing 'state of the art equipment and cutting edge facilities', was opened to provide both academic study and hands-on vocational learning for 16 to 18 year olds. Part of the process is to work with local businesses who help to mentor students and provide work placements. The school was recently described by Ofsted as 'outstanding'.

School Art Class 1920 (Archbishop Holgate's School)

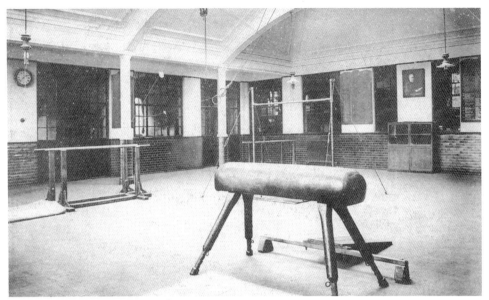

Gym 1920s (Archbishop Holgate's School)

Richard Nihill teaches at Archbishop Holgate's comprehensive school and is the lay chaplain.

I work with the vicar of Heslington Church. I arrange workshops and resources for form tutors and have periods of reflection. I arrange services and it does include pastoral work, when there's been a family issue or a family separation or in times of bereavement. We have a school chapel, paid for by the old boys. It's used for lunchtime clubs and assemblies and voluntary services every month. There are some external counsellors who come in to use the chapel because they find it a nice, calming space.

York is twinned with the diocese of Cape Town. I went to visit South Africa in 2004 with a group of teachers from different schools. We've taken three groups of pupils over there. We do educational work but also community work, painting and gardening in an orphanage, we've raised £6000 for a classroom for a poor township pre-school. It's part of what we're about as a school in terms of charitable work.

NUNTHORPE GRAMMAR SCHOOL

After the First World War, the only boys' secondary school in York, Archbishop Holgate's, had become overcrowded. The headmaster applied to the local authority to build further extensions but instead the York Education Committee decided to open two new schools, Mill Mount Secondary School for Girls and Nunthorpe Secondary School for Boys. Both were located in the Scarcroft Road area of the city. Nunthorpe Court was a fine Victorian house built by the Atkinson brothers in 1856, and a few decades later was the home of Colonel Sir Algar de Clifford Charles Meysey-Thompson, baronet. When the school took possession, his son Ernest Meysey-Thompson moved to live at the Lodge, at the bottom of the impressive avenue of lime trees which leads up to the school, where he died aged 81 in 1967. The Court was bought by York Council for £10,750, opening in 1920 with 49 boys, of which 27 were fee-paying. The first headmaster was R J Evans, and the first pupil to be listed in the register was Kenward Allen of Balmoral Terrace, who was born in 1907.

Nunthorpe Court was situated in attractive grounds, which included a formal Italian parterre, sloping lawns and an artificial lake. On a clear day the White Horse on the distant Hambleton Hills could be seen from the top floor. Also in the grounds stood Nunthorpe Hall, built some years after the Court, described by English Heritage as 'one of York's most lavish Victorian houses, with a sumptuous interior, looking out over the Knavesmire'. Before the First World War, the house belonged to Sir Edward Green who allowed it to be used as a hospital during the war. It opened in October 1915 with 50 beds, with a convoy of men direct from the battlefield of Loos, and closed in 1919. In May 1916 it was bombed during a Zeppelin raid which

Nunthorpe Hall 1865 (Darrell Buttery)

caused damage to part of the house and grounds. The Hall was eventually converted into 16 flats and demolished in 1977.

An article in the Old Boys magazine of 1970 by 'MHWP', describes the early

Nunthorpe Hall as hospital in 1915 (Mike Race)

days of the school, 'Nunthorpe Court was crammed with sporting and military trophies of its owner, a retired colonel. There was no electric lighting, only open fires for heating. The most vivid memory is of a large wooden hut erected to augment the teaching space, where those at the front roasted and at the back, in bad weather, the ink froze in the ink wells'.

Initially equipment was scarce with only chairs, tables and blackboards. Woodwork had to be taught at the nearby Scarcroft School. The assembly hall/gym was added in 1927 by roofing over the stable yard, and this later became the dining room. By then, the pupils totalled 280, with 39 in the sixth form. A new wing was completed the following year, with four classrooms, an art room and cloakrooms, forming one side of a quadrangle. A tennis lawn was laid out, the stables were converted into laboratories, and the stable-boys' sleeping quarters became the library. By 1932, there were 468 boys.

By 1929, in the York City Year Book, Nunthorpe was offering 'a thoroughly sound secondary education, such as will fit boys for either professional or commercial careers'. Fees were £5 5s a term. The quadrangle was completed in 1937, with workshops and a hall, and later a rose garden was added, being donated by parents in memory of boys killed in the Second World War. In 1959, a new block with laboratories and more classrooms was built, together with a gymnasium. The Parent Teacher Association financed the school bus, trampoline and other games equipment.

Godfrey Fowkes was born in 1918.

In September '29 I went to Nunthorpe. Classes were organised into A, B and C forms according to the level of intelligence. I was in 3A, 4A, Lower 5A and Upper 5A. Then I took the School Certificate and left the school in 1933.

Going from a primary school to a big secondary school was quite daunting. But you came to fit in and enjoy it and I was very happy. The headmaster was Mr Hampson [from 1927 to 1930], *followed by Walter Seville. Mr Hurworth took Latin, Mr Foggin took maths, Mr Molloy took history. Mr Peckitt took geography and sport, Mr Pragnall was music, and the woodwork master was Mr Stratford.*

They had a playing field and a couple of football pitches. I wasn't interested in ball games but I was fond of gymnastics. I used to attend special classes at the Railway Institute in the evenings. I belonged to the school boxing club but I'm not going to say I liked it, I did that to please my father. In summer we went to Rowntree's Baths for swimming, although as this was chargeable, I tended to use the River Ouse quite a lot. I also enjoyed cross country running out to

Class of 1930, Godfrey Fowkes is fifth from left on front row next to Mr Wright, French master
(Godfrey Fowkes)

Bishopthorpe. We once went to Edinburgh by rail, did a tour round, saw the castle and the Royal Mile. I remember the trip back because we schoolboys were having a crafty smoke.

Godfrey does not recall boys smoking at school, which would have resulted in major punishment.

You weren't allowed to leave the school grounds but we'd nip over the wall to a little shop nearby and buy pies and sausage rolls. That's about as far as we got for being naughty. I made a lot of friends and we kept in touch but we were all dispersed at the end of the '30s when the war came. I know one or two who didn't come back.

I think we always felt that Archbishop Holgate's was a better school. It had more of a tradition about it. On the other hand, the education at Nunthorpe was better. You could go to Nunthorpe by paying fees, but I didn't, I got the scholarship. You had to live within the city boundaries for that to apply.

My favourite subject was history and I was also fond of languages. When I left school, the headmaster gave me a reference.

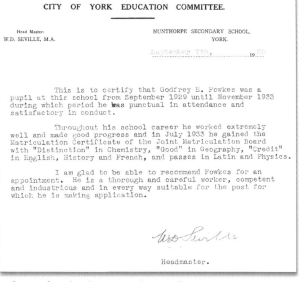

CITY OF YORK EDUCATION COMMITTEE.

Head Master:
W.D. SEVILLE, M.A.

NUNTHORPE SECONDARY SCHOOL,
YORK.

September 7th, ...19....

This is to certify that Godfrey E. Fowkes was a pupil at this school from September 1929 until November 1933 during which period he was punctual in attendance and satisfactory in conduct.

Throughout his school career he worked extremely well and made good progress and in July 1933 he gained the Matriculation Certificate of the Joint Matriculation Board with "Distinction" in Chemistry, "Good" in Geography, "Credit" in English, History and French, and passes in Latin and Physics.

I am glad to be able to recommend Fowkes for an appointment. He is a thorough and careful worker, competent and industrious and in every way suitable for the post for which he is making application.

Headmaster.

Reference from headmaster Walter Seville (Godfrey Fowkes)

Godfrey also recalls that one of his classmates was Freddie Graysmark, who became a drummer with local dance band Ray Archer and the Modernists. The band practised in Clifton and Freddie would cycle from his home in Wilton Rise, Holgate, with the drum kit in pieces attached

French play early 1930s. Front row - ?, Mr Wright, French master, boy with black face is unknown, Robert 'Pop' Over, French master, ?, Mr Hurworth, Latin master, Walter Seville, headmaster, Mr Stratford, woodwork master, Mr Pragnall, music master, ?, Austin Foggin, maths master, Mr Oldfield, history master. Godfrey Fowkes is immediately behind Hurworth and Seville (Godfrey Fowkes)

to the bike, and the bass drum on his back. In the 1930s, one of the most popular dance bands in York was the Rialtonians, who won a number of contests and made several recordings, on the Octacros label. The band had its beginnings in 1927 when four members were in the sixth form at Nunthorpe. Len Cundall played clarinet and alto saxophone, as well as string bass, Jack Potter was the drummer, Leslie (Curly) Cowell played trumpet and George Barnes played piano. The band entertained troops in Africa during the Second World War. In the school magazine in 1980, George wrote,

We still get together from time to time to have a blow, 53 years after first playing together at a school concert in the assembly hall at Nunthorpe.

School clothing advert
(Millthorpe School)

John Dale attended the school in 1933.

Rialtonians 1938 winning county championship cup. Nunthorpe boys include Len Cundall, being presented with cup, George Barnes on right, Jack Potter behind (with moustache), Leslie 'Curly' Cowell (York Oral History Society)

I remember the utter charm and grace and beauty of Nunthorpe. They had lovely Italian gardens and a beautiful parquet floor. In the main building, the glass dome was above and central light played onto that floor. They had bas relief figures on the walls, everything was painted. There was a stone balustrade outside about eight inches wide and it went round the corner and ran up the windows over the pediment. The boys used to walk along it, for a dare, when you got to the upper fifth.

Meysey-Thompson lived at the cottage at the bottom of the drive. He always carried a dispatch case and umbrella and wore a bowler hat, a very military man. When Lycett Green had Nunthorpe Hall, Edward Prince of Wales [later Edward VII] *used to visit and have a tryst there with Lillie Langtry.*

I was lucky at Nunthorpe because of a master called Kneebone. He suddenly opened a door and there was Shakespeare. If you've got a good teacher you're there, if you haven't, you're lost. It's difficult to break through later on, because you get lazy mentally, say, "It's not for me", and you leave it.

Nunthorpe Cricket First XI 1933-4. Captain is Burdett, headmaster Walter Seville is 3rd from right, with 'Pop' Over on his left (Millthorpe School)

During the Second World War, at least 133 old boys served in the forces and over 40 were killed. Nunthorpe had an Air Training Corps, with over 100 members. Teacher (and old boy of Archbishop Holgate's) Francis Jameson, aged 32, of Leeman Road was killed in the 1942 air raid on York, and the school accommodated Queen Anne's girls two afternoons a week after their school was badly damaged. In 1945, the kitchen at Nunthorpe

Nunthorpe production of Merchant of Venice 1935 (Millthorpe School)

was hit when a Halifax aircraft crashed on a house in nearby Nunthorpe Grove. By this time, the school had 500 boys. After the 1944 Education Act, Nunthorpe became a Grammar School.

Dr Ian Stead recently retired as Deputy Keeper of Prehistoric and Romano-British Antiquities at the British Museum. He attended Nunthorpe in 1947 following junior school at Poppleton Road.

Nunthorpe Prefects 1953. Back row L to R - ?, John Nicholson, ?, Douglas Klein, Peter Fowler. Middle row – Billy Lamb, Howard Cox, Brian Miles, ?, Alistair Murray, Ian Stead. Boy in middle of front row is head boy. (Millthorpe School)

That's what Vince Cable [the Liberal Democrat Minister] *did too, he went to Poppleton Road, Nunthorpe and Fitzwilliam College at Cambridge, so he followed in my footsteps.*

At Poppleton Road, you were very much pushed and you did all these questions, [11 plus practice papers], *not education, it was getting you through exams. We were told that at Nunthorpe there was 'the wall', and you would get pushed off 'the wall' and other horror stories. That was one of the surprises, there wasn't a wall and nothing happened like that.*

You got very bright people there. I was always interested in history and we had a very good master, called Whittaker. He'd been an economics teacher at Hull University and had come back because of the war. And I enjoyed art. I got thrown out of music because I was doing a caricature of the music master and he swiped me over the head and said, "If you're so good, you can spend every music lesson in the art room". So every music lesson I trotted along to the art room and picked up my canvas and had a whale of a time.

Nunthorpe Art Room 1950 (Millthorpe School)

[In 1951] *we got a new headmaster,* [Mr Moore]. *After you'd taken the School Certificate, under the old headmaster we were allowed to go out and play cricket or muck around for a fortnight. This new fellow announced that when we'd finished taking the exams, we would do library work. That went down like a lead balloon. It was at that point that an archaeologist came to the school, Peter Wenham, and said he was doing an excavation at Trentholme Drive, and wanted volunteers. This was the way out. There were four of us. We went down and saw this site of a Roman cemetery. And there were all these students scraping away at skeletons and we thought,*

"This is the life". Then he took us to the other side of the road where there was an enormous bed of nettles and he wanted a trench digging so we had to clear the nettles, we found the remains of an air raid shelter, concrete and whatnot, we had to get rid of all that, dig this great trench and at the end of it, we found nothing at all. He said, "Excellent, that's negative evidence. The cemetery mustn't have extended as far as that". But next year he offered to pay me so I went and worked with him at Blossom Street, on the Roman Road. That's how I got into archaeology.

Peter Wenham (foreground) and Ian Stead excavating at Riccall 1956 (York Archaeological Trust)

I was interested in sport. I actually played for the school Second XI at soccer and I ran in the cross country. We had a very good geography master called Hurworth, an inspiring teacher. He said that what you really need to do is to read the Observer, which was very good advice in those days. The other thing I really enjoyed was the Boy Scouts. I got more out of that than out of school, education rather than passing examinations, getting on with people and having responsibility.

In the sixth form I started an archaeology club and we produced a newspaper and had an exhibition. The prefects used to lord it over the young lads. One of the main jobs we had was making sure that everybody wore a cap outside school and you had to take names of people who weren't. All pretty dreadful, I didn't like that at all. Our new headmaster decided that we ought to be getting far more people into Oxford and Cambridge. He got six or eight of us and put us in for open scholarships, the most difficult way of getting in. One of ours got in that way and another two got exhibitions, but I didn't.

I had a great friend called John Nicholson, he'd always been passionate to go to Cambridge. He was a member of an organisation called the Crusaders, he went on one of their camps and somebody there said, "You've got to write to the Censor of Fitzwilliam House". He was invited down for an interview and given a place. I thought, "Just a minute, all these flaming exams that we're taking and terrible interviews and he just walks in". So I wrote off, and went down and the Acting Censor told me, "The only problem is whether to read archaeology or history". Archaeology was so narrow, they were keen you should read history and get a broader education. But I said, "I'd like to read archaeology".

I trotted over to the Department of Archaeology and Graham Clark, the professor, was busy digging. "Could I see an archaeologist?" All the archaeologists were out. "How about an anthropologist?" "I suppose you could see Mr G I Jones". He was sitting at his desk writing some learned paper and hardly looked up. "What do you want?" I explained the problem. "What the hell do you want to read?" I said I wanted to read archaeology. "Well go away and read bloody archaeology then". So I trotted back to Fitzwilliam House and said the Department of Archaeology had recommended I read archaeology. "Right, can you come up next October". I went back to school and Mr Moore the headmaster was very pleased and was going to work out a programme of research in the library, but I said, "Actually I've got a job, starting in January". He was furious that I'd done this without asking permission. George Willmott at the Yorkshire Museum had offered me a job as a museum assistant for £2. 10s a week. It was Peter Wenham who pointed me in the right direction.

Nunthorpe had a large number of societies, including yachting, astronomy, photography, debating, climbing, bridge, birdwatching, bee-keeping, electronics and a club which built a hovercraft in the 1950s. Nunthorpe claimed that it 'sets out to develop boys on all sides – intellectually, imaginatively and physically'.

Tim Kjeldsen was born in Swansea in 1953 and is now a teacher and practitioner of the Alexander Technique.

Tim Kjeldsen aged 13 (Tim Kjeldsen)

I'd done one and a half years at a technical grammar school in Nottingham and then we moved to York. I suppose I'm ideologically in favour of comprehensive education, it seems a good thing for society that everybody gets educated together. But at that time I probably thought that grammar schools were superior. I think it's important to try to bring out the best in people. The difficulty is to provide a broad enough range of possibilities, so that children with very different kinds of abilities have them nurtured and supported. The secondary modern schools were supposed to be state of the art institutions offering vocational education, but they ended up being schools where kids who didn't have the ability to get to grammar school, were dumped.

Nunthorpe retained a kind of ethos that it had probably had since the war. There was a culture of order that you just slotted into. Everything was under control. It was a protected and safe environment. If you fitted that mould, it was actually very rewarding. The problem is that not everybody fitted it. It was unjust and society can't tolerate that without an enormous strain.

His favourite subjects were English and history.

I did belong to the drama society, from about the fourth form. We used to do shows with Mill Mount, which is probably why I belonged to it. We went to Stratford and to other theatres. We started a magazine too. I think it would have been better to have been at a school with girls, but it was quite a privileged life, a good breeding ground for a professional career. They knew how to get you through exams, so most kids did really well and got good places at university. The balance was different then, there were more old teachers and they were more effective. The younger teachers did try to bring in new ideas and to relate to the boys but some were unable to maintain discipline. I remember a young maths teacher who was newly qualified and very committed, full of a kind of imagination but could not get the respect of the boys. We used to run riot in his class, so I had two years of wasted maths. He eventually went to Africa to teach. I thought about him a lot, I realised how motivated and dedicated he was but he wasn't able to handle groups of boys. Then I went into a more orthodox maths class and actually began to learn a bit of maths. With the teachers with the more traditional approach, it was clear, you knew what the rules were and as long as you obeyed them, they were fine. These guys had got it sussed. They knew how to do it, they were good at it and it wasn't difficult for them.

THE MILL MOUNT—NUNTHORPE DRAMATIC SOCIETY

Mill Mount-Nunthorpe Dramatic Society (Millthorpe School)

We did have characters. I remember Pop Over, called that because he was always 'popping out'. He was a gentle sweet man, and the first aid officer. There was an incident on the rugby field, and Pop would pop out of class and you'd see him walking across the rugby field with a glass of water and a couple of aspirins. He wasn't very agile. It took him a long time. All the boys would be looking out of the window and cheering him on.

The assistant headmaster was called Jewels. We called him Jimmy. He was the one with the cane, he would go round terrifying the life out of people. But I never remember anyone getting caned. It would be detentions and lines and having to pick up litter for talking in class or climbing on the roof to get a ball.

Mr Jewels was the ultimate mechanic. He'd dictate notes, we'd write them down, take them home and copy them into our best books. That was our history, there was no engagement with it whatsoever. The geography teacher was Mr Peckitt. We called him Flaff because he had a flaffy moustache. He'd write things on the board and leave gaps and

Ernest Norman Jewels, deputy head at Nunthorpe 1960s (Millthorpe School)

you were supposed to look up in text books to see what the gaps were and fill them in. Some of the older teachers did have eccentric forms of discipline, humiliating boys was an easy way of maintaining control. They could be quite scornful. A pretty destructive thing to do. I remember some bullying incidents. There was a boy who was off school for a long time. I was summoned to the headmaster's office and asked, "Are you aware of anyone using sharp instruments? Will you look out and see if you can see anything?" And indeed there turned out to be. I went back to the headmaster and told him, which was probably the right thing to do. I felt slightly mixed about it, they thought I was either trustworthy or could be manipulated. But sometimes with bullying, there was the feeling that this was between the children and the children had to sort that out, this was part of their growing up. For boys, it would have been seen as weakness if you had to run to your parents. That was nothing to do with the educational aspect of the school. The school taught you the subjects, kept you disciplined and what you did in the playground was largely up to you. It wasn't particularly unpleasant, just tedious. If you had a lively enough mind, you could absorb stuff, memorise what they told you and you passed your exams. That was the deal and you could get on with the rest of your life.

For Tim, the school suddenly changed as he reached the sixth form in 1969.

We were part of the '60s generation that thought it was changing everything. We had very relaxed relationships with the teachers, even socialised with them to some degree. We were treated as young adults. Nunthorpe might have been rather narrow by modern standards. I felt generally supported and cared for by the teachers. On the whole they treated us with respect.

One of the reasons I was happy was because it played to my strengths. In the sixth form I began to discover the pleasure of study. The most important memory I have was the first class in English with Arthur Harrison. There were 12 of us in the class instead of 36. He took his chair from behind his desk, sat in the middle of the room with us, it was all incredibly deliberate, and proceeded to talk about the Elizabethan world view. My jaw hit the floor and I was astounded that people could look at the world in different ways, it was a moment of revelation, an epiphany, a turning point in my life experience. I remember that vividly, and the passion with which he talked, the enthusiasm, and the breadth of his own interest and engagement with the world. He was a very reflective individual and he shared that with us. A good teacher is somebody who really does want whoever they're teaching to flourish and develop. He was the person who really did change my life.

Sadly, Arthur Harrison died suddenly at the age of 61, whilst walking in the Lake District. He had been Head of English for 24 years.

My experience in the sixth form started my interest in theatre. That's why I ended up doing a degree in theatre at Dartington where I met the Alexander Technique. What I like about it, is that there's a kind of intellectual dimension to it which I find very stimulating and exciting.

The 1970s brought many changes. In 1970 the new headmaster, Geoff Cushing, arrived, with a new deputy head and several members of staff to replace those who had retired. Sixth former Andrew Briggs began to build a yacht, in which he later sailed round the world. The roll of pupils reached 780. A new sixth form block was built in 1974, which is today used for science labs and language rooms, and the computer arrived at the school in 1976. That year, teacher Tom Bardy left to be head

Arthur Harrison on left at Nunthorpe
(Millthorpe School)

of biology at Bar Convent. He had been assistant PE teacher and in his 15 years at Nunthorpe introduced rugby union, rugby league, and judo. He took charge of basketball, helped start up a camp in the Lakes and helped coach some of Britain's international athletes. He played scrum half for York Railway Institute rugby union and professional rugby league for Dewsbury. A knee injury meant he retired from sport in 1970 but he continued to coach.

The school magazine was a vehicle for news, especially of sports and other achievements, but also for creative writing of poetry and prose. It is interesting to compare an issue from 1945, which had poems about 'The Eskimo' and the life of a caterpillar, with those from the 1970s with poems about existential angst, suicide, and the end of the world.

In 1977, Ernest Norman Jewels, deputy head, who had taught from 1957 to 1970, died at the age of 72. He was involved with 20 productions of the Nunthorpe/Mill Mount Dramatic Society, and had met his wife Joyce Metcalfe, a teacher at Mill Mount, through this. A memorial fund in his name was set up for old boys and, in 1978, a memorial seat at the school.

Darrell Buttery is well-known in York, as President of York Civic Trust. He was born in Guisborough, studied history at Durham University, and came to teach English at Nunthorpe in 1974. Old boys speak of Darrell as a very inspirational teacher.

I wanted a career in journalism but life has peculiar ways of operating and it didn't come about. Instead it was a career in teaching that went on well after retirement. Nunthorpe was a superb school to teach in, marvellously good fun, a fantastic staff, terrific academic record, and great sporting prowess. It was focused on educating boys to the best of their ability, giving them a very good start. Even though it was a very happy school, it didn't stop people losing their temper. It didn't stop ear tweakings and blackboard chalk throwing, slipperings and canings. Nowadays young teachers are cosseted and made to feel welcome and important, they're monitored and trained. In the old days, you qualified and came into the classroom and that was that.

If you had problems with discipline, the big boys would move in and sort out your class. Now we are obsessed with monitoring and measuring. A lot of energy goes into that and it has in some ways stifled creativity.

You worked to the exams for the senior forms. Other than that, you chose what you wanted to teach. One of the greatest strengths was that we took in a large number of pupils at sixth form level. Hearing from teachers in secondary modern schools, if they found pupils who wanted to learn and were academically bright and who'd failed the 11 plus, they gave them such attention, they could develop at the pace they needed, and they were nurtured and a number went on to Oxbridge. Some of those pupils would have been lost in a comprehensive school and would not

Darrell Buttery, English master 1980s
(Millthorpe School)

have got the level of care that the smaller secondary moderns gave them.

There was a lot of drama, always very enjoyable. I remember a festival in 1975. It started well with a zany take-off of a rock group, but after a while the audience became restless. I had kept what I thought was the best play till last. Richard Taylor and Timothy Shaw's group gave a splendid parody of a Sherlock Holmes play which was to end with some shaving foam custard pies being pushed onto the faces of the principal actors. All went well till the last scene when a table appeared covered in pink blancmanges. At this point, hysteria was beginning to set in. First one, then another, was squashed by willing hands into joyful faces, the audience on their chairs with excitement. Then Richard asked whether anyone in the audience would like one. They had arranged for one boy to volunteer. They hadn't guessed that 50 hands would go up and boys would jump on stage and hold their faces tantalisingly ready. Within seconds pink blancmanges were flying everywhere, and by the time I got on stage, it was all over. The stage had turned pink, the curtains were sky blue with pink dots, and even the piano looked like some giant dessert. It took ages to clean up, mainly because the boys seemed to think that the more water they put on, the quicker it would go. I had to reorganise the cleaners in getting rid of, not lumps of trodden-in blancmange, but a pink swamp. When I got home, my mother had prepared blancmange for tea!

Darrell enjoyed taking his architecture club on various visits, including the state room at the Mansion House.

The butler was a little agitated by our late arrival but the boys soon sweetened him up. Then he showed us the new display case of silver whilst the boys asked their usual offbeat questions like, 'What would happen if I put a brick through the glass?'

On April Fools' Day, there were a full quota of things balanced precariously and obviously on doors. I retaliated by setting homework

with poker faced
deliberation, 'Write an
essay on being made
an April fool of'. The
cleverest prank was
during the changeover
of periods. With skilful
arrangement forms
mixed their classrooms so
that I for one did several
laps of the quad before I
found my lot. Form One
seemed to think that

First formers in Darrell Buttery's English class, 'being a double decker bus' c1979 (Darrell Buttery)

April Fools' Day meant acting the fool so that half of them greeted
my arrival by sitting on chairs on top of their desks and singing the
National Anthem.

One out of school activity which Darrell led regularly, was a camp in Helmsley,

*with our PE master and 16 first formers. We went on an eight mile
walk through the woods and there was a great spirit among the boys.
[Two of them] walked across the river fully clothed and others were
feverishly tugging at shoes and socks and rolling up trousers. We
came upon a paradise, a large area of closely cropped grass bisected
by a shallow stream. The boys whooped with pleasure and were soon
absorbed in all the activities boys find to do in streams. They even
fished, pulling from the water quite large specimens. We walked by
the river for a mile or so, stopping when it was dusk to have our
supper and build a camp fire. Andy Burks found a wooden cross and
pretended to be St Joan. When he later started to run through the fire
as a game, I said we'd have to be returning. The boys loved exploring
and came back with a standard assortment of boys' treasures – peeled
sticks, feathers, rusty penknives, rock samples and dead rabbits.*

Another event in school was the Mock Election.

The whole school packed the hall to hear the speeches from the three
pupil candidates. Each one spoke well, but the Liberal had some of
the best lines. He called for higher teachers' salaries and was greeted
with boos. But then he told the crowd that the staff had to remain
not involved since, as in the general election, criminals and lunatics
were not allowed to vote. This brought the house down.

Darrell recalls a winter scene when

the trees were pasted with thick hoar frost so that Nunthorpe looked
like the palace of the Snow Queen. The sixth form had discovered
the joys of sledging on bits of plastic and broken tea trays and by
lunchtime the slopes were thick with activity. I took my skis along
and found I could go quite a way on them, particularly if I used them
almost like a sledge.

I took the second form to see the Heath Robinson exhibition in the
Art Gallery. They were in one of their mischievous moods. I had some
business in King's Manor and as I came over, I heard a loud speaker,
I thought it was a police car until I heard, 'Calling Mr Buttery'. Paul
Harker was shouting down the plastic cones the police use to stop
parking. I took them to see the 18th century pictures. Half of them
sprawled out as if they were on the living room carpet until I tidied
them over to the ledge at the side, whereupon a custodian appeared
and shifted them again.

In 1980, Darrell gave a sherry party for

all 13 of our Oxbridge candidates, the highest number in the history
of the school. They were a splendid group and I felt proud of them.
Andrew Martin was accepted to read history at Merton. He was an 11
plus failure and came in the sixth form. I remember thinking 'What a
nonsense that selection exam is!'

One of my tutees, a delightful sleepy looking boy we used to call Dormouse, became national karate champion and was photographed with a cup that looked as big as himself.

In 1982

we went to the Assembly Rooms for the Evening of Dance. The boys looked resplendent in their military uniforms. Matthew Abel and Glenn Wintringham were dressed in authentic footmen's uniforms once belonging to the Stourton family, quite magnificent. Beneath their powdered wigs they wore white coats festooned with gold braid, and black velvet breeches with white stockings. They recreated a feeling of the gracious past more than anyone

Matthew Abel and Glenn Wintringham dressed in livery of Lord Mowbray of Stourton. *(Darrell Buttery)*

else there. The boys danced very well especially Malcolm in the polka. On the way out I complimented him on keeping so close to the girl. 'I had to', he said, 'I'd got my foot stuck in her dress'.

Darrell remembers a visit with sixth form boys to the studio of painter John Langton who,

talked about his days at Nunthorpe in the 1940s and hit the boys' wavelength immediately with his slightly irreverent, dry humoured approach. He spoke of the brilliance of the sixth form. "You were expected to work and in consequence lots of us spent time in town".

He told them about the Stonegate café, and they listened fascinated. "We colonised it and spent whole mornings there. The seriousness of it was extraordinary as was the unspoken agreement to educate ourselves". When John went on to talk about painting, he threw out so many challenging statements. He explained some of his paintings which was an education in art such as I've never had before. "In painting the image stays still and the mind moves".

During his time at Nunthorpe, Darrell proposed the idea of a Junior York Civic Trust.

I thought I'd gather a nucleus of keen boys and start a group with Mark Kesteven, Rupert Griffiths, Ian Shannon, Glenn Smith, Michael Webb and Richard Gledhill. We met at the Cemetery Chapel and they were as taken with its atmosphere as any adults I've shown round. The point was to show them the sort of problem the Civic Trust would involve itself with, and to enlist their help in recording inscriptions.

Rupert Griffiths went on to teach and is now head of St Oswald's Primary School. A keen historian, in the 1977 school magazine he also wrote about York Archaeological Trust and suggested setting up a Nunthorpe Archaeological Society. He asked, "In a city like York, isn't it disgraceful, if not impossible, not to take an interest in the past?"

Rupert Griffiths 1978 in Nunthorpe school magazine (Millthorpe School)

Today Nunthorpe has its share of well-known old boys, including Charles Whiting, military historian and author of over 350 books mostly about the Second World War, (he left Nunthorpe at 16 in 1942 and joined the army by lying about his age), nuclear physicist Doug Cline, politician Vince Cable, Mark Addy, actor of 'Full Monty' fame, and Steve McClaren who was captain of the school football team, before turning professional at the age of 18 in 1979. He retired in 1992 after an injury, and was manager of the England team from 2006-7. In May 2010 he became manager of Wolfsburg, the first Englishman to manage a German football team.

The last Nunthorpe headmaster, Geoffrey Cushing, retired in 1984 to become lay pastor at Southlands Methodist Church. In 1985 Mill Mount came to join with Nunthorpe to become Millthorpe Comprehensive School, with pupils from other schools joining subsequently. The school now accommodates 1000 pupils.

Nunthorpe Badge (*Millthorpe School*)

– CHAPTER 4 –
Grammar Schools For Girls

Queen Anne's Grammar School (York City Archives)

QUEEN ANNE'S GRAMMAR SCHOOL

Queen Anne's began life as the Municipal Girls' Secondary School at the Brook Street Pupil Teacher's Centre, behind St John's College in Lord Mayor's Walk. One pupil described it as 'a chilly and gloomy building, without a cloakroom, without a kitchen, without a library, without a gymnasium, without a garden. But there were classrooms warmed by an open fire, a hall where we danced at recess. There was a draughty corridor on which to hang coats, a gas-ring where we boiled milk, and a laboratory where jellies were made at festive times, with the help of beakers and Bunsen burners'. By 1907, a new school was designed by Walter Brierley and built in Queen Anne's Road. It was opened in January 1910 by the Archbishop of York, with 219 pupils, becoming Queen Anne's Secondary School. The first principal, Mr H Rayner, was replaced by one of his eleven assistants, Miss Emily Netherwood, later that year. The number of girls increased so much that the school had to temporarily use 70 Bootham in 1919, and the local authority decided to open a new girls' school, with half the girls and some staff, moving to Mill Mount Secondary School for Girls in 1920.

Headmistress Miss Netherwood (in centre) and staff 1920s (York City Archives)

Queen Anne's School Zoo 1950s (York City Archives)

The 1938 York City Yearbook advertised Queen Anne's as 'a well-planned modern secondary school, with laboratories for chemistry, botany and physics, a domestic science wing, library and extensive playing fields. Fees £4. 4s per term'. In the first year girls took deportment and learned to walk the length of the hall with a book on the head. In the gardens, girls planted hundreds of crocuses amongst the rose beds and in the early spring, after prayers, Miss Netherwood would say, "We will take a crocus interval", and the whole school went out. She retired in 1938 and was replaced by Doris Milner, with Joyce Aspden taking over in 1942.

From 1948 the school had its own zoo, with budgies, rabbits and various other pets and insects, and had rotas for cleaning out and feeding them. In 1960 York was officially twinned with Münster in Germany, although some individual exchanges had been made before that. In 1970, came the twinning between York and Dijon, and Queen Anne's, along with other schools, got involved in pupil exchanges over the next twenty years.

Queen Anne's Hockey team c1910 (York City Archives)

Queen Anne's Netball team 1920 (York City Archives)

Queen Anne's girls gardening 1910 (York City Archives)

The last headmistress, Miss Irene Whittaker, came in 1960, and took the school through to its final days as a grammar school. She was awarded the OBE in 1984 for her work as co-chairman of the Joint Council for National Criteria for the GCSE examinations. From 1972 Queen Anne's was used as the Saturday morning York and District Music Centre for children from all over the city. In the 1970s came the advent of Activities Week, which the grammar schools held in order for pupils to do something completely new for a week, such as sailing, marine biology, stage costume and make-up or developing photographs. In 1974 there were extensions built, with a three storey block which included a 36 booth language laboratory, new physics and chemistry labs, music and drama departments and a new library. In 1984 more building work took place to adapt the school into an 11-16 co-educational comprehensive.

Mary Barr was born in 1927.

When I was ten I got a scholarship and I chose Queen Anne's. It was part fee paying and part scholarship. I remember mother taking me to kit me out, to Isaac Walton's in Coney Street. You had a velour school hat, blazer, gymslip, blue and white patterned blouse and a tie. I had to learn to tie a tie, I had never done that before. I think it got a bit funny at times, but I was quite proficient at it before I left.

Mary Barr at Queen Anne's School, fourth from left on front row. c1940 (Mary Barr)

There's one thing I didn't like at the school. Nowadays the girls wear shorts for games. We had to just wear our navy knickers and I can remember going down to the hockey field and seeing all these faces gazing at these girls, and I did not like it. We had netball and tennis courts, and a hockey field lower down. In winter it got flooded.

The school did sometimes flood when the river rose, and later in the bad floods of 1982, those taking exams had to do so at St Peter's. One member of staff reached school by canoeing across the tennis courts, and mooring outside the music room.

Floods at Queen Anne's Grammar School 1947 (York City Archives)

I liked English and acting. The mistress had a most delightful lisp and she was very good at acting. I loved art. I think it was kindled by our art mistress Esther Walker. [Mary later became an artist and has done a number of commissioned paintings]. *Miss Netherwood was a delightful lady too, she was lovely.*

They built an air raid shelter, on the left hand side as you look down the school towards the river. Queen Anne's was bombed [in April

1942, five heavy explosive bombs were dropped in the grounds]
*and in the netball courts was a great big crater. I remember the
form room with glass all over the floor, it was an awful mess. I was
as shattered as the glass. The next day they were using the dining
room for people in Queen Anne's Road who were bombed out of their
homes. All the windows had been broken. We could only use certain
rooms because we were taking our School Certificate. The rest of the
school was not allowed to go in.*

There were also doors ripped off their hinges, window frames swaying
precariously, holes in the roof and plaster everywhere. The girls helped
elderly people in the area to clean up their houses. The road had been
badly affected and the next morning a rescue squad was still at work
digging for buried occupants. Another old girl recalls, 'Six of us went to
the British Restaurant, peeling carrots and potatoes, and washing dishes
until we were tired out. It was good to see the bombed-out people
enjoying their meal, some with bandaged heads or hands'.

*I went through to the Lower Sixth but I'm afraid I was very naughty,
I decided to leave after the Christmas. I wasn't unhappy but I
wouldn't say it was the most delightful time of my life. I had much
more fun after. But you've got to be educated otherwise you can't get
on.*

*I left because all these other girls were having a nice time, going
to dances, and I couldn't because I was doing work. I did my*

CHRISTMAS.   *The Magazine of the Queen Anne School, York.*   1937
Magazine Committee :
Editresses : Ruth Stratford, U.VI ; Peggy Bell, U.VI.
Business Representatives : Joan Morritt, U.V. ; Joan Reynolds, U.V.
Staff Representatives : K. H. Wake ; R. G. Scott ; W. Tindle.

The Sphinx, Queen Anne's School magazine 1937 *(Mary Barr)*

hairdressing apprenticeship and eventually had my own business, the Regency Hairdressing in High Petergate. I did the hair of several teachers, and Irene Whittaker got me to go back into school and talk about it.

When my daughter was going to grammar school in 1975, we went round Queen Anne's and Mill Mount. I got the impression that Miss Whittaker was very much 'for' comprehensive education.

Mary was not happy with this idea.

It holds the brighter ones back and the presence of the brighter ones doesn't encourage the poorer ones, just makes them feel left behind. So it makes them care even less.

I liked the attitude at Mill Mount so we decided on that for Carolyn. The man who coached for Oxford inspired her to read physics at university. They were having a netball match between the staff and the girls and he dropped down dead while he was playing. [This was Derek Cockroft who died at the early age of 40]. *Miss Cook* [the Mill Mount headmistress] *suggested it might be an idea to have a term at St Peter's and take the Oxbridge exam from there. She got five A levels at Grade A. Then she left at Christmas because she got the offer of a place at Harwell, the atomic research place, they only gave 12 places to pupils in the UK.*

Brenda Milner went to Queen Anne's in 1940.

I think most of us in our area did go to grammar school. People from secondary schools thought we were above ourselves. I was

Brenda Milner 1939 (Brenda Milner)

very impressed with the school, it had beautiful parquet floors in the assembly hall and mahogany doors. Some of the classrooms had a balcony looking down onto the lovely gardens.

I liked geography, history and we had a domestic science section where we took one term doing needlework, and the first thing we made was a huge pair of knickers, then a cookery term and then more general things like learning how a range worked.

Then there was a dreadful time, it was terribly windy and there was a row of elm trees between the tennis courts and the hockey field and one blew down and a girl was killed, Joy Websall. One of the group came running up and we realised there must be something wrong. She ran to the staff and said the tree had blown down, there was a girl underneath it. They shouted, "Come on, all of you", to try and get this tree off her, but she was dead of course.

During the war there were many restrictions. At the end of each term, the girls had to polish their desks and provide their own Brasso to clean the brass lids of the inkwells.

After the bombing, while they were repairing the school, we went alternately to Nunthorpe and Mill Mount. We loved going to Nunthorpe but they kept us away from the lads. We had speech day at the Salvation Army hall. In wartime a lot of the London orchestras and plays weren't performing in London and they came to York. We certainly did go to concerts, 'The Marriage of Figaro', Gilbert and Sullivan, and the D'Oyly Carte did 'Iolanthe'.

We had dances during the lunch hour, usually with a girl playing the piano. For music we had Miss Lenton. They'd have Wings for Victory weeks, and we took part in the choir and went to sing outside the Mansion House. When we sang hymns, we had to pronounce the end of every word, very clipped. Later on I've been with people in a service, and they've said, "I bet you were at Queen Anne's. You sound the same, the way you all sing".

Queen Anne's Speech Day at Salvation Army c1948 *(York City Archives)*

*The head, Miss Milner, was a Ukrainian. There was a bit of a
mystery about her. I'm told she was very strict with the staff. The lady
who taught French taught us well, but she used to say, "You girls
will drag the name of the school in the mud". But we all passed. In
1942 Miss Aspden came. She was really ladylike, and was a Quaker.
She was very insistent on us giving something back to society. We
had three streams in each year, A, B and lower. And suddenly there
was a change and we took the initial of our form mistress, to make
everybody appear equal. We did things for the Youth Service and went
to visit old ladies in hospital who'd been evacuated from London.
We went potato picking during the autumn holiday. A retired history
teacher, Miss Pressley, set a competition in the Easter holidays, about
the history of York, and finding names of streets. So that kept us
occupied, in and out of the reference library, it was fun and probably*

set me off on an interest in local history. They asked one Christmas
if any family would take a French airman from Elvington for
Christmas dinner. One family did and the girl eventually married the
Frenchman.

We wore panama hats in the summer and a blazer trimmed with
white cord and a sphinx badge. The school outfitters were Isaac
Walton's, Southcott's in St Sampson's Square and Miss Matterson's
down Goodramgate. You could make them too, there were set
patterns. We had a different form room every year and we looked
over the railway that runs from Marygate and there was a lad we
knew at St Peter's. On the afternoon when he was on his way back, a
girl next to the window started coughing loudly to tell us David was

Queen Anne's Staff 1942. Back L to R – Mr Caughie, Miss Segar-Smith, Miss Barton, Miss Sycora,
Miss Haigh, Miss Harris, Miss Waterson, Miss Prentice, Alice and Mrs Thompson, domestic staff,
the gardener. Middle row – Mrs Noble, Miss Wheldon, Miss Miskin, Mrs Kirkup, Miss Tindle,
Miss Shone, Miss Swaby, Miss Cleland, Miss Wake, Miss Walker. Front row – Mrs Holmes, Miss
Halmshaw, Miss Horton, Miss Skerry, Miss Milner, headmistress, Miss Boyd, Miss Deans, Miss
Karfoot, Miss Barnard. Seated on rug at front – Mrs Fish, secretary, Mavis Hemmingway,
lab assistant   (Brenda Milner)

Matterson's School Outfitters
(Mary Barr)

on his way back to school. I don't think anybody cottoned onto that, just thought she had a bad cold.

On VE Day, there was an ice cream firm on Lawrence Street whose daughter was in the school, and I remember him sending ice cream for everybody.

Brenda's father was killed at York Station during the night of the Baedeker raid in 1942.

I hardly remember anybody mentioning it. Perhaps they'd been told not to talk about it. [Today she would be offered counselling]. *My mother was a widow and I had to get a job. I thought she wasn't going to let me take School Certificate. But I did and got seven credits, and two passes. I went to the Yorkshire Insurance. They expected you to be ladylike there too. Workers called each other Mr or Miss.*

Brenda became Lady Mayoress of York in 1985, and recalls the school reunion.

It was the year the school stopped being a grammar school, so I invited the ones from my year to the Mansion House. After that, they said, "We've got to keep together". Now we meet three times a year.

Queen Anne's School Reunion 1989 of Form VY 1940-45. Back row L to R – Mary Davies, Dorothy Kirk, Monica Boynton, Dilys Roberts, Eileen Birch. Middle row – Barbara Smith, Anita Tacey, Brenda Milner, Audrey Davies, Pat Glensor, Mavis Boulton. Front row – Sheila Shackleton, Margaret Gould, Josie Wright, Liela Try, Irene Dawson (Brenda Milner)

Girls from Queen Anne's did go into careers, travelling or undertaking higher education. Many taught in the USA, Canada and other parts of the world. Winifred Yates became the first Principal of the Gnanodhaya Training School in Madras, and Josephine Stancliffe was Sister in Charge of the Ruanda Mission Hospital in the Congo in the 1960s, and 'played a leading part in preventing the tribal massacre of 300 Africans'.

Queen Anne's became a comprehensive school in 1985, but closed in 2000 and the property was sold to St Peter's School.

Fancy Dress Day (including wartime outfits) 1942 (York City Archives)

MILL MOUNT GRAMMAR SCHOOL

Mill Mount House was built in Mill Mount Lane off The Mount, by York architects JB and W Atkinson, in the mid 19th century, for Charles Heneage Elsley, a county court judge and recorder of York from 1834 to 1865, who died at the house in 1891. His daughter lived in Mill Mount Lodge until her death in 1925, but Mill Mount House was bought by the Walker family. There is a moving memorial in Holy Trinity Church, Micklegate, to Captain Edwyn Walker who died in 1919, his wife Elizabeth who died in 1915, and their four sons - Edwyn Walker, barrister of Inner Temple, killed in a point to point race in 1910; Captain Oswald Bethell Walker of the 15th Hussars, killed during the retreat from Mons in 1914; Major Wilfrid Beckett Walker, of the 1st Yorkshire Regiment, killed at Ypres in 1914; and Captain Roger Beverley Walker, MC, of the Yorkshire Hussars, killed in the 'Great Advance' in November 1918. It was erected by their only daughter and sister Dorothy Katharine Brewis, who lost both parents and four brothers in nine years.

Walker Plaque in Holy Trinity Church, Micklegate (Van Wilson)

When Mill Mount Secondary School opened in the house in 1920, little work had been done to convert the elegant family home into a school, mainly because of the lack of resources. An anonymous ex pupil, writing in the Yorkshire Evening Press in 1960, recalled that, 'The girls worked in bedrooms decorated with lush wallpaper, climbed stairs lined with ruby damask, and rooted out exciting finds, like the cockaded top hats of the former coachman and footman in the old coach house. They relished science classes in the cavernous gas-lit kitchen, with a vast cooking range big enough to roast an ox'. The family's dining room became the gymnasium (later the Upper Sixth common room), the butler's lobby became the prefects' room, the drawing room became the hall where girls knelt for prayer in assembly, and the owner's private study became the headmistress's office. The beautiful terrace and rose gardens have always been an important feature of the school.

The only laboratory was in the former billiard room, the basement was occupied by wine cellars, and an army hut was divided into three classrooms. The chemistry lab was introduced in 1922 and the cookery centre in 1925. The first headmistress was Josephine Burne, who started with six staff, and several peripatetic teachers who took music, art and needlework. She was paid £500 per year, and the other fulltime staff were paid between £197 and £250. There were 104 girls, many from Queen Anne's School.

Miss Burne resigned in 1927 at the age of 46 and was succeeded by Miss Nicholls, who had come from Queen Anne's and taught previously at Cheltenham Ladies' College. She devoted

Mill Mount Grammar School entrance
(York City Archives)

herself to building up the reputation of the school and attached great importance to academic achievement. In 1928, of the 24 girls who left school, one went to university (the first to go to Oxford), four to college, seven took clerical jobs, three worked in shops, five worked in other jobs and four stayed at home. (By 1983, 37 went to university, eight to further education, four to train as nurses and the rest into jobs). There were eight prefects, a thriving literary society and a history society called the Old York Chroniclers. The four houses were named after important women – Astell (Mary Astell, 18th century advocator of equal educational opportunities for women), Bronte, (the Bronte sisters, 19th century novelists), Fawcett, (Millicent Fawcett, suffragist who struggled to improve women's opportunities for higher education in 19th century) and Somerville (Mary Somerville, Scottish mathematician after whom the first Oxford women's college was named).

By 1933 there were 272 girls. A new wing was added to the old house in 1935 with an assembly hall also used as a gymnasium, showers, changing room, cloakrooms, four classrooms and a biology lab. An additional playing field was provided at Nunthorpe in 1938 but without a pavilion, so coats and hats had to be hung on a wooden fence.

Nancy Dawson attended Mill Mount in 1933.

We played netball and cricket and I captained the junior rounders. We had a game called longball, a tennis ball was delivered by the bowler and you hit the ball with your hand, then ran the length of the pitch dodging the fielders who would try to catch the ball.

Mill Mount Class 1930s (*York City Archives*)

They let me work at Mill Mount for the last year in the chemistry and biology laboratories. If they wanted an experiment putting up, I'd do it ready for the class, and when they'd finished I'd take it down and clean all the vacuum flasks. I would also clean out the tanks. There was a butcher in Nunnery Lane and I used to hate going there to ask for a pennyworth of meat to feed the two damn terrapins. I wasn't a lover of reptiles but it was my job. I did a tank out one night with two newts but they must have slipped down when I took them out to clean the tank. Don't ask me to this day where them two newts went but I never did find them.

With the advent of the Second World War, uniform regulations were relaxed to some degree. The navy gym tunic was still worn, with the braid girdle. Fawn wool or lisle stockings could be worn owing to the difficulty in obtaining black. The white summer hats could be dispensed with and cyclists could wear navy woollen 'pixy hoods' on windy days, or navy berets on wet days. Girls also had to provide white Tootal poplin blouses, dark blue overcoat, navy science overall, indoor, outdoor and PE shoes.

Vera McHugh started at Mill Mount in 1940.

In the main entrance there were boxes for the air raid shelters, with biscuits, a bottle of water and first aid kit. One of the jobs I did was to collect these and take them to the shelters. We had to carry gasmasks everywhere and your outdoor coat rolled up in an American cloth bag, with shoes and your books. If the siren went, you might be caught between the old building and the shelters, so you had to go and sit on the spiral staircase [in the old house] *because there was less glass to fly around. The windows were covered in coarse netting, as in buses, so if they had broken, they wouldn't splinter. When we went back to school in the autumn of 1945, it had all gone, the windows gleamed, it was wonderful, I'd never seen the lovely views you got over the Knavesmire.*

View from Mill Mount over Knavesmire
(Christine Kyriacou)

Everyone was expected to do Youth Service. We wore a white badge with a black Y on it, and if you did so many hours, you got a red binding tag. You wore this with pride. Collecting rosehips became the fashion because there were no citrus fruits and rosehip syrup was a good source of vitamin C. And we went unpacking mugs at the station. They regularly disappeared, when soldiers took them on the trains. So when a new consignment came, a huge crate was dumped in the concourse opposite Smith's bookstall. We'd unpack them, get rid of the straw, and wash them. That was a nasty job because straw got everywhere. They had Holidays at Home, and we'd volunteer to go to Acomb Primary School and supervise rounders. We helped when ration books had to be reissued each year by the Food Office and if we had a double period of English, a pile came and we filled in the names. We also made socks and balaclavas of the most awful coarse wool for the troops. The staff had to fire watch in the old building because they had access onto the roof which was absolutely forbidden to us.

Most of the teachers were dedicated spinsters. If you got married, you automatically lost your job. But during the war quite a lot came back to teaching and there were lots of supply teachers. We'd get an 'assistante' for French conversation. Miss Mutch taught German and we still had textbooks with the old German gothic script. Miss Kordik came in 1943, she took maths. [She became deputy head in 1959 until she retired in 1973. When she died in 1990, a commemorative fund was set up in her name].

Miss Easton, who taught English, was a rather cold, distant lady, an Oxford graduate and very clever. She was keen to improve your vocabulary so you did lots of exercises with words like 'sporadic'. At Christmas, she would read from Dickens, 'Christmas at Dingley Dell' with Mr Pickwick, and she read it so beautifully, it seemed that much funnier. The only male was the music master, Mr Pragnall, who used to do concerts in St Helen's Square, for Wings for Victory. We sang songs like 'Land of Hope and Glory', and 'I Vow to Thee my Country'. The Settlement on Holgate Hill hosted meetings for the French air force [based at Elvington]. *We'd learn French songs and their national anthem. That was the spirit of the times.*

There was always the problem of not having enough space. We used a field near Nunthorpe and played hockey in our gym vests and knickers. Then a rule came in, that that was okay on your own home pitch where no-one could stare at you. They found out that Nunthorpe sixth form, there was a balcony and they used to go out and watch. I don't suppose they knew for quite a time what the attraction was.

Next to the old house, they had ovens, and the boiler house. There was a little pantry and a dumb waiter that went into the dining room upstairs. We found out that this pulley arrangement was still working so somebody would climb into it [and ride up and down] *but they soon put a stop to that. All the old loos that belonged to the maids' quarters, were still there with the old-fashioned crazed glazing.*

School milk at break time 1950s *(York City Archives)*

School dinners were heavily subsidised. A dinner ticket was fourpence a day, the same price as the British Restaurant in town. They had lightweight plastic tables with American cloth, stacked near the cloakrooms on the ground floor. There were eight to a table. If you were on duty, you had to rush down, put your tables up, go into the kitchen and collect eight glasses and a jug of water. Some meals were pretty foul. Fish pie used to be called 'shipwreck', 'the piece of cod that passeth all understanding'. The stew had too much gristle. But Mrs Biggins' [the cook] rissoles were very good. In cookery, we made steamed puddings in tiny dishes, and vegetable soup, the most awful grey stuff, no chicken stock cubes, just vegetables. My friend's mother said, "They're not worth fourpence, don't bother to bring it home".

The first year needlework was all hand sewn and we learnt French seams, and how to darn socks and do a right angle rip darn. We made aprons, very poor quality. One yard of material and you had to cut it out, and make the pocket and straps.

We did drama in the sixth form. I was Hermia in 'A Midsummer Night's Dream'. I think there were about 30 of us. You had to be really good and confident to go to university. I was 15 when I took

School Certificate, and then did the Higher Certificate at 17 and went to London to teacher training college.

Vera later taught English at Burton Stone Lane School and Acomb Secondary School.

By the end of the war, Mill Mount girls had raised money for causes including the Red Cross Prisoner of War Fund, China Relief Fund and the County Hospital. They sent toys, blankets and clothes to children in Greece, helped at rest centres, collected books and paper for the city's salvage drive, toys for bombed-out children, helped to entertain in old people's homes, and acted as messengers for the air raid wardens.

With the 1944 Education Act, Mill Mount became a grammar school and pupils no longer paid fees. The last head, Dorothy Cook, explains that,

during the war, meetings were held about what would happen to education after the war and one of those was in Mill Mount, in about 1942. The education minister came with all his entourage.

Joan Campbell went to the school in 1949.

I think the 11 plus is divisive, and a lot fell through the net. I've been told they had a different standard with boys and girls. The girls were probably more ready at 11. It was a crucial point of your life to stream you in that way. If they got it right, and I think with my brother they did, by going to a secondary modern it gave him time to mature, he got a good grounding and went on to do an apprenticeship, that suited him. But for other boys, they didn't get the chance to go to grammar

Rita Day, Pauline Allatt and Joan Read (now Campbell) 1950s, garden of Mill Mount. (Joan Campbell)

school and it curtails your career and stops progress. The thing that came out from Mill Mount was an ability to cope with what was coming. I might not understand a particular thing but I can learn and then can do it. That is a great thing in life and when I was doing the Open University many years later, you think, "I'm just as capable as they are. There's no big deal here".

Our teachers were practically entirely middle aged, middle class single ladies and we thought they were ancient. They had a different view of life which was a bit narrow. I suspect they were essentially academic, always been bright, never had to struggle. Some teachers knew their subject well enough but couldn't make it 'live' for the pupil, therefore you shut off and thought, "I don't like this". I'm convinced it's in the hands of the teacher as to where you go and it was sink or swim. If you were struggling and you became disinterested, that was your hard luck. A bit of encouragement might have made a huge difference.

Miss Willoughby [who had become the third head in 1946] *was a very smart lady and a good setter of standards and someone*

Miss Willoughby and prefects 1952 (*York City Archives*)

you admired. But you wouldn't have wanted to go to her and say, "There's a problem at home". They were unapproachable in that respect.

Some of the teachers were human, quite a few you felt were on another planet and didn't have any understanding of the girls. They would be completely unaware that a lot of girls had no father in the house, we're talking about a few years after the war. You got the impression that a bright girl who couldn't stay on, her earning power was needed at home. If someone was an only one, the father had a good job, the child went to university, but there were others who were just as capable who didn't do that well. You think, "Why didn't they say that you could go to work and do A levels at evening class, and apply for teacher training?" But where did we go? Railway offices, Rowntree's, Terry's offices, Yorkshire Insurance, the banks, a lot of which were boring jobs I have to say.

The vast majority didn't stay on into the sixth form, they left with O levels, [introduced in 1951]. But you hadn't finished your education then, everybody I knew went to evening class or day release. By the time you'd got to O level work, they were tightening up. They didn't take a personal interest. You were just told you weren't good enough to take the subject. When the exams finished, there was no syllabus to follow and the staff were so much nicer. I remember having a history lesson out on the lawn and going off on our bicycles to one of the villages.

School occupied the greater part of a girl's life.

You got home at 20 to 5, had tea, did your homework, listened to the radio, knitted, sewed or read, and went to bed. At weekends we'd go to the theatre, I remember doing homework on the steps going up to the gods.

Discipline was quite heavy. They were very keen on how you presented yourself. If you were fooling around in the street, someone would see it. And eating in the street was absolutely taboo. A bus would arrive

Outside the headmistress's study at Mill Mount (Christine Kyriacou)

and everybody wanted to get on and somebody would say, "A lot of hooligans", and that would get back to Miss Willoughby. Nice girls didn't answer back and that was the norm. One or two girls in my group had babies out of marriage, they were adopted. There was a home in Heworth Green, which was where girls went. It's desperate when you think about it, it's cruel. You were all so scared and naïve.

The '50s were not the best years for girls in education. Universities and training colleges took relatively few girls. But even though you came out of Mill Mount with a handful of GCEs, the majority of girls have made a success of their lives. It was good confidence building, you imbibed the ethos and general feel of the place. It raised your sights, rather than in some schools, where, if you were bright, you were stamped on and you don't want to reach your potential because you are looked on as a swat. I am proud to have gone there. If you'd been to Mill Mount School or Queen Anne's, an employer knew what he was getting.

Joan is involved with running the Mill Mount reunions.

Even if you weren't a close friend with someone, the bonds are still there. When you've gone through that period of your life and have that in common, it stays with you. You really value those friendships.

In 1959 another new wing was built with gymnasium, art room, classrooms and laboratories. There was a school canteen with domestic science rooms on the other side of Mill Mount Lane. New playing fields were provided at the bottom of West Bank in Acomb. By 1964 there were over 600 girls and 36 staff.

In the 1960s Mill Mount was the centre for the Nuffield Physics Project, and also took part in a project which assessed English Language work throughout the year rather than having exams, an experiment which spread throughout the country.

Joyce Cockerill (née Mason) went to Dringhouses Primary School and to Mill Mount in 1964.

Joyce Mason 1970, is in central row, fourth from left
(Joyce Cockerill)

I loved primary school, it was quite a shock to move. Suddenly you go to a school where there's lots of people you don't know, it seems big and scary. I remember the first day vividly. We had to wear berets. As I was walking into school, I was grabbed by some older girls who pulled my bobble off, and made a hole. It was the thing they did to all new first years but it was quite upsetting when you're walking into a brand new school.

The form teacher was Miss Parker, she taught maths. She seemed very old but was such a lovely person. Miss Willoughby was very revered. The worse thing possible was to be summoned to her office. She was fair but very much old-school with discipline. There were strict rules about the length of your skirt, which way you had to walk down a corridor, and about being quiet. You had to stand up when a member of staff walked into the classroom. The teachers fell into two camps, staff who seemed very old because of the way they dressed and the way they were, and younger people coming in who dressed and acted differently. My cookery teacher, Mrs Owen, was always approachable. When I was going to college to Alnwick, she said, "You'll like it there, I've got family up there". But if I was inspired by anybody it was teachers I'd had at primary school.

We weren't allowed to go in the main entrance, that was for staff only, they went up quite a grand staircase. There was a huge area of grass and a greenhouse which we used for art lessons, tucked away at the back of the old house.

I liked English and cookery, and loved geography. But you didn't discover things for yourself. You were just told. Somebody stood at the front and wrote things on the board which you had to copy down. I don't think anybody ever questioned what a teacher said. There was never any place for discussion. School is better now because they become more independent and their opinions count. They have a better relationship with their teachers. We didn't have a relationship. A teacher came into the classroom, taught the lesson and went out.

A lot of people say the discipline's gone now because you haven't got this strict regime we had. But we behaved because we were frightened of the consequences. The way they learn now is a huge improvement. We were never taught to think, just given facts. If you weren't very good at remembering facts, and

Mill Mount Conservatory *(York City Archives)*

you didn't understand it, you couldn't work it out.

In the sixth form we were given more freedom. There was a sense of responsibility and that we'd made it to the top. I became a prefect, it mostly meant being on duty at the changeover of lessons to make sure people moved around quietly. For A level I did geography, English and RE. We organised a party in the sixth form, like today's prom. We all made long dresses and felt very grown up. That was really special.

It was good to get rid of the 11 plus because it favours people who are good at doing tests. If you all go to the same school, you can find your strengths and weaknesses. You might be in the top group for one subject but further down in another. Now they come out as much more rounded people.

Domestic Science 1950s. Maureen Chevens is fourth from left with mixing bowl (York City Archives)

There were many changes in the 1970s, including the advent of the School Council with a representative from each form, and the decision to abolish the infamous school berets. In 1974, the senior games mistress, Maureen Chevens, who was one of only three women to be both pupil and mistress, (along with Audrie Parker and Marjorie McKay), left the school to move to Ireland. She had been a pupil from 1948 to 1955. She had learnt to swim at the age of nine and joined the York Swimming Club, training several nights a week and on Sunday. Later she swam for York Schools and Yorkshire Schools, and was county champion in the 100 yards freestyle for five consecutive years. In 1950 she was part of the

Yorkshire and Lincolnshire division of the first All England Schools Swimming Championship in London, and we came away with two of the trophies.

She was selected for the Olympic training weekends but feels that,

I was up against people who were better than I was. I turned my attention to the teaching side of swimming. I took the ASA swimming teaching certificate at Mill Mount and the Advanced Teaching Certificate when I was at college. So I went in that direction.

TEMPERATURES

Boiling point of water is 212° Fahrenheit.
Oven Temperatures.

Desired Temperature	Electric	Gas—Mainstadt	Regulo
Very Hot	475—500	G—H	7—8
Hot	425—450	F—G	6—7
Moderately Hot	375—400	D—E	4—5
Slow	250—300	B—C	2—3

TO TEST OVEN TEMPERATURE WITHOUT A THERMOMETER —
A hot or brisk oven.—The hand held in the hottest part of the oven (usually the top) should sting at the end of a 9 or 10 seconds count. A piece of kitchen paper placed on the top shelf for 3 minutes becomes a rich chestnut brown.
A moderate oven.—As above but the paper becomes a pale golden brown in the same time.
A slow oven.—Paper does not colour.
A small portable thermometer can be bought at reasonable cost; its use will prove helpful when learning to judge oven heats where no regulator is supplied.

Northern Schools Cookery Book 1940s (Christine Kyriacou)

Choosing a career in teaching meant she could not take professional swimming any further, or pursue the next rung on the way to the Olympics. After several years of teaching in Nottinghamshire, she returned to Mill Mount in 1961 as Senior PE mistress. Her other great love was Scottish country dancing. She started a club after school and was also involved in the city club. Today she is still involved in country dancing and still swims.

In 1980 the school's allowance was cut by 7½ per cent and the library allowance was lost. But there were more opportunities for trips, whether locally to Fountains Abbey, Helmsley, and skating in Bradford, or to London, Edinburgh and the Isle of Wight. There were canoeing and fell-walking weekends, and in 1983 the first joint Mill Mount and Nunthorpe trip, to Austria for skiing.

Some of Mill Mount teachers 1970, Maureen Chevens far left, Marjorie Mckay far right, both were originally pupils (Joyce Cockerill)

Mill Mount teachers 1970 L to R – Miss York, Miss Patchett, Miss Parker, Mrs Duckworth, Mrs Horne, Mr Pettigrew (Joyce Cockerill)

Marie Wood, head of modern languages, retired in 1980. She was awarded the Medal of the City of Dijon in 1968 as she had spearheaded the school's twinning and was invited to advise the BBC on French school broadcasts.

Trip to Dijon 1952 with French teacher, Marie Wood on left (York City Archives)

The fourth and final headmistress, Dorothy Cook, took the school from 1966 through to its closure in 1985, and was President of the York and District Head Teacher's Association. She was also on the panel for borderline cases in the 11 plus examination.

There was basically a number you could take but you had to allow for mistakes in choosing, there was that area of greyness. We had to get at what the child could really do. We'd choose sections of books which we knew children could manage. 'The Borrowers' was one. We'd ask them to read, and asked them questions. Then we tried to get them to talk about their interests. We tried to make it friendly and relate it to what they knew. What really struck me was the little boys who knew so much about fishing and things like that.

> *There are some people who don't show at eleven. At 12 or 13, you get*
> *a far better idea of what people are capable of. My own feeling is that*
> *it would have been better to have primary school, middle school and*
> *13 upwards. You'd have got the sixth forms within the system. But*
> *people say that it is more expensive.*

In November 1982, the first interest was expressed by the Catholic
authorities in taking over Mill Mount to couple with the Bar Grammar
School. Miss Cook was appointed head of the new comprehensive which
would amalgamate Mill Mount with Nunthorpe at the latter site and, after
one year, pupils from Knavesmire, Ashfield and Danesmead also came in.
She was the only woman to head a comprehensive at that time.

> *At my interview in 1966, I was told there were plans for*
> *reorganisation so throughout that time there were uncertainties. I*
> *know some parents were not happy. The tension was certainly there.*
> *The new heads were appointed first, in 1983, and they, with the*
> *education officers, interviewed people, to see how they compared with*
> *others and how people's different wishes fitted in. You had to get the*
> *balance of grammar and modern.*

> *It was difficult. I was running Mill Mount for the last two or*
> *three years, and at the same time trying to get Millthorpe off the*
> *ground. We had no extra help. I had a monthly meeting with heads*
> *of department and we thrashed out quite a lot and staff did get to*
> *know each other, which helped. Miss Whittaker was retiring, and*
> *Mr Cushing [from Nunthorpe]. It was essential that Millthorpe*
> *was going to get off all right. Having got everything we could sorted*
> *out, about a week before Millthorpe opened, they discovered a major*
> *gas leak in the science lab. We had to alter a whole lot of things.*
> *I remember one of the workmen saying to me, "That will last a*
> *hundred years". All I was interested in was getting the school open.*

> *There were some people who quite definitely didn't like*
> *comprehensives and regarded it as looking forward to retirement, but*
> *there were others who really opened up and thought this was great.*
> *If you've been used to a fairly easy grammar school life, to meet with*

*both boys and girls, that upset some people. I know one or two staff
who said they weren't going to teach boys.*

*For the first two or three years, more of them were from grammar
school, but we did have others,* [from secondary moderns] *and it
was obvious that some of them settled in really well and blossomed,
once they came to a comprehensive. We had joint meetings of parents
and they chose the name Millthorpe.*

Miss Cook's whole career was in teaching, with over half of it as a head.

*I can't think of anything else I would rather have done. But when
I was a head it was very different. It's far more a management
thing now, concerned with money and not the same opportunity
for teaching and getting to know people. Things have got more
prescriptive, there's definitely less freedom.*

*One thing I feel quite strongly about was the support that teachers
need. Mr Thompson and Mr Richardson,* [the caretakers] *made a
real difference, and an efficient secretarial staff makes a tremendous
difference. If these things get cut out, it does lead to less efficient
teaching.*

Miss Cook retired from Millthorpe in July
1988 and received an honorary degree from
York University in 1990.

In preparation for the removal of Mill
Mount, an inventory of school property
had to be taken, which was a colossal job.
In the chemistry lab alone there were 106
Bunsen burners, 156 retort clamps, 24
mortars and pestles, 107 safety goggles, 30
reflagrating spoons, 97 glass conical flasks,
19 bell jars and 212 evaporating basins. The
drama department had its lighting, scenery,

Dorothy Cook (*York City Archives*)

curtains, wardrobe and projector. The art department had radial easels, heating rings for batik, drawing boards, weaving looms, potters' wheels and kilns, and aluminium whirlers. The PE department had the most equipment and all of these had to be distributed to other schools and the school made ready for All Saints' Upper School to move in.

All who speak about the girls' grammar schools, mention how they embodied very high standards, and taught their pupils to behave like young ladies. Strong values were instilled into pupils from the early days, and were well established by the time of the third head, Margery Willoughby, always known as Twill, who retired in 1966. She had studied history at Girton College, Cambridge and when she died in 2001, aged 95, a close friend spoke, at her funeral, of her high standards and recalled the last meal she had prepared for him, with 'an immaculate linen tablecloth, Waterford glasses, bottle of hock, pheasant and all the trimmings, then strawberries served on deep green Wedgewood plates which had belonged to her grandmother'.

THE BAR CONVENT

Bar Convent 1930s (Image reproduced courtesy of City of York Council, Local Studies Collection)

The Bar Convent is the oldest living convent in England, established as a girls' boarding school in 1686, in a building close to its present site on Blossom Street. The latter was bought in 1766 by the first Mother Superior, Frances Bedingfield. At the time it had to be established in secret. The nuns flouted the law and built a beautiful chapel, hidden from the outside. In preparation for raids by magistrates, it had eight exits and a priest hole, though some nuns were caught and imprisoned. The convent also opened a day school in 1699, and was granted a licence in 1791 after the Catholic Relief Act permitted Catholics to worship publicly. The building was extended in 1844 and the architect G T Andrews was also responsible for the glass roof, a beautiful feature over the central court, now the main entrance. During the First World War, the convent took in Belgian refugees, and part of the building became a hospital ward. In 1921, the day school and boarding school were amalgamated and in 1929 the direct grant system came in. In the Second World War, tragedy struck when five nuns were killed during the Baedeker Raid of 1942, when a bomb hit the convent. In 1977 the school became the Bar Grammar School and started to admit boys, firstly in the sixth form and then throughout the school. In 1985, although nuns remained in the convent, the Diocese of Middlesbrough took over running the new Catholic school, All Saints.

Sheila Goater was born in 1923 and attended the Bar Convent prep school in 1929.

Sheila Goater (marked) at Speech Day 1934 in Concert Hall (Sheila Goater)

Originally it was a totally private school, It was founded by the Institute of the Blessed Virgin Mary founded by Mary Ward. She thought that girls should be educated and was very much disapproved of by the Vatican. Eventually they were accepted. They bought the property and started educating the daughters of the local gentry. The nuns still live in one part. St Bede's Pastoral Centre [next door] is run by the nuns, an education centre. There were separate houses which they bought over the years. Most of the teachers lived in the school.

In the 18th century the school as it is at present began to take shape with new buildings replacing the original house, with many more

rooms with connecting corridors and stairs. In my day the corridors were highly polished and we were severely reprimanded if caught sliding, always a great temptation. In this complex of rooms we were never sure which would be our classroom at the beginning of a new year until 1936 when a new wing of four classrooms was built extending into the garden. In history lessons, the name of Mary Ward was often mentioned. She had never seen the opening of Bar Convent but her spirit was there.

Plaque of Mary Ward outside Bar Convent
(Christine Kyriacou)

At 11 you went up into the senior school and girls came from the other [Catholic] schools in York, St Aelred's, St Wilfrid's and St George's. There weren't many non Catholics. In my class there were three or four. They weren't made to go to religious classes, what they called doctrine. The non Catholic children used to sit at the back and do their homework. We rather envied them. The classes were Lower Three, Upper Three, Lower Four, Upper Four, Fifth form and then Lower and Upper Sixth.

There were lay teachers too. Mr Franklin, the music teacher, I think he was assistant organist at the Minster. The whole ethos of the school is practising the religion. There was a lot of emphasis on good

*behaviour, which emanates from your belief in humility and the
ten commandments and faith, hope and charity. We used to have a
retreat every year, a whole weekend of prayer.*

*Attitudes make all the difference in teaching. History was my
favourite subject and English literature. The history teacher became
the head and she wasn't the same at all. When people get authority,
they change. I spent three years in the sixth form, I was only 15 when
I took the School Certificate. For Higher School Certificate I did
French, English, geography, Latin and history, two main subjects and
three lesser subjects.*

*The only ones you felt were slightly favoured were the boarders. They
had to look after them like mothers. I shouldn't think they had more
than ten in the whole school.*

*I was there for eleven years. It's the growing up part of your life, it
has a big impact on you. When you refer to anything, you refer to it
in terms of school for a long time afterwards. It comes back to you
when you get older. Our class joined the Old Girls' Association and
we went once or twice, I started going again in recent years.*

*Most of the girls left after School Certificate. A very small per cent
went to university.
I don't know of
anybody going
before 1929. There
were three of us in
Upper Sixth. We
went to lectures at
St John's. I think
the school was very
encouraging, gave
you confidence.*

*The processions
are the things I*

Procession from St George's Church c1933 (York Oral History Society)

The War Convent School, 1.8.C.M.,
York.

Programme for Speech Day

Wednesday, 1st December, 1937

Speech Day 1937 *(Mike Race)*

remember most. They used to be in the city. In the summer there was a procession which started at the Poor Clare's Convent on Hull Road and we walked to St George's Church and had Benediction, then we walked back and they have a great big garden there and we had another service. We used to sing hymns all round. That was for all the parishes. And another procession about Easter from St Wilfrid's Church, over Lendal Bridge, down Rougier Street and up to the Shambles, past Margaret Clitherow's house and back to St Wilfrid's. Then they had an open air mass in the Museum Gardens and the monks from Ampleforth used to come and say the mass there. We went in white dresses.

Although Sheila trained as a teacher, she did not go into teaching.

I did history as a main course and archaeology was involved with that. I went to London to work in a social work centre, and moved after six months to the Ministry of Economic Welfare. I got very interested in archaeology. York Archaeological Trust started, and I suggested we talk to schools to encourage them to come and look at the digging. I started going round to schools for 20 something years, getting the Trust known. I went all over, within a hundred miles of York, giving talks, and I'd meet schools and take them to particular digs. It was very interesting.

Sheila Goater at York Archaeological Trust 1977
(York Archaeological Trust)

The education I had has had a big influence on my life. I don't feel like falling away from the church as some people do. Everything I've done has led me to where I am now. I can see a sequence and they've all helped me to enjoy what I do.

June Lloyd-Jones (née Prendergast) also went to the prep school and up to the senior school in 1940.

It was a private school so I just went straight through. But we did get a lot of girls coming from outside. The boys went mainly to St Peter's.

It did come to a point when they had to put an embargo on and say they couldn't take any more non Catholics, which was a pity because I was always a champion for them, I think the Catholics probably got favouritism. When it came to wartime, we got quite a lot of girls from further south.

June was there when the blitz of 1942 hit the school.

I remember going back and seeing the whole of the middle part where the nuns lived had been hit. One of the nuns, they tried to get her out but she was right where there was a ticking bomb and that did go off. We lost five nuns altogether which was pretty awful, a huge loss. Some of us did go back to help with cleaning up. [The bomb] hadn't affected the actual school

Bar Convent after Baedeker air raid on York April 1942 (York Oral History Society)

except very much emotionally. It was hard to go back again. After that, a lot of lay people came in. I still write to one of the nuns, she taught history and geography. She must be coming up to 100. I remember her saying that she'd worked in Mesopotamia. And I thought Mesopotamia was the most fantastic, magical word.

You had to have your gas mask if you went to play on the Knavesmire. You had to share plimsolls because there was a shortage. We had to cut up old car tyres and stick them onto plimsolls we already had. My mum had a sweet shop at the front of the Rialto [June's father owned the Rialto cinema], *so I could get various sweets and a proper tray to carry them in and I started at break time selling them and another girl did it with me. We were doing a roaring trade for a couple of weeks until one of the nuns saw us. But I was complimented on my foresight, seeing a niche.*

Sometimes when the weather was bad, the winters were so awful, I remember having to wear a long coat of my brother's, right down to my ankles. Sometimes you had to walk because of the roads, nothing got cleared so it was like walking on an ice rink.

I was in detention lots of times. I went out with a boy from Bootham. And another girl was going out with a boy from there and we got pulled over the coals into the headmistress's room and asked when we were getting married. We looked at each other in total amazement. You got a whole group who were going out with boys who delivered telegrams. One girl was crazy, she didn't give a damn, just a mad person. It's lovely to have somebody like that. Always in trouble, most days something happened, going into parts that they weren't allowed to go into, and being generally a nuisance.

You got different nuns who would be all right with you and others who wouldn't and others who had their favourites. I think a lot went to be nuns because they lost the men they were going to marry in the First World War. I remember in the Second World War our English teacher coming in very quietly, and someone said, "Her fiancé's been killed", and she never married.

Members of Institute of Blessed Virgin Mary Society at Bar Convent, June Lloyd-Jones is third from right on front row. c1945 (June Lloyd-Jones)

Some of the nuns were incredible, like Mother Aquinas [the head]. *I think my life changed with her. She always understood. When I left, having done School Certificate, she put on my report, "June deserves to succeed". When someone puts that, it cheers you up.*

There were strong friendships. It's quite incredible, they do last. The majority of girls were absolutely super. I can't think of anyone who wasn't nice to get on with.

I loved English, and art of course, we did have good teachers for art, [June is an artist] *and geography. I went back to teach art for a couple of years. It isn't like teaching and you can just encourage people. There was one pupil and they said, "She can't do this and she can't do that". And I saw real potential in her. At the end of term, we had things put up for parents' evening. There were two girls in front and they said, "Ooh look who's done that. And she can't do anything at all". But it was a lovely picture.*

Main Hall at Bar Convent 2010 (Rob Maw)

Occasionally if someone was on leave, I filled in, and they said, "Mrs Lloyd-Jones how come we do such a lot of drawing in your history lessons?" I said, "I think it's the best way I can get you to enjoy it".

If you love something, I don't care what it is, if you can do that with a child and encourage them, it means such a lot. You feel pleased even if you've encouraged just one person along the way, it's an exciting feeling.

Edna Scott had a different experience at the Bar Convent, partly from being a non Catholic. She went to Naburn village school, and was the only one in the family to pass the 11 plus.

We were the Golton girls. There were five of us, and Naburn was only small so the Golton girls made up the village. We went to Methodist Sunday school and every year they did an anniversary where you recited or sang a solo. We used to say to the vicar, "Don't say our surnames. We don't want people to know we're all one family". But we all looked exactly the same. We were very poor. My mum made all our clothes without a sewing machine but they used to say "she turned them out spick and span."

I was allotted to Bar Convent in 1957. There were only three non Catholics in my class. I wasn't happy. Right from the word go, you felt alienated. All the girls knew the Catholic religion, and the catechisms off by heart and I didn't have a clue. I remember going home and crying and my mum sent a letter saying I hadn't to learn it. It was a school I didn't really want to be at, the wrong religion. There were poor kids there but they were Catholics and that seemed to make them part of the fold.

The first year I found very hard but I put my head down and worked. I was third in the class out of 31. But after that I didn't want to work, I rebelled against everything that was going. The nuns were all right, the other teachers were quite nasty. The headmistress Sister Thomas was strict. You couldn't talk in corridors. We were going to lunch one day. The staircase up to the chapel was a dark little place. I

Chapel at Bar Convent 2010 (Rob Maw)

was talking and this hand came out and grabbed me on the shoulder and I screamed. [It was Sister Thomas]. *I got detention for weeks and weeks, on a Saturday morning. I used to bike from Naburn and tell my mum I was playing hockey, I couldn't tell her I was in detention. She was struggling to pay for school uniform without her daughter being an absolute idiot.*

The thing that stands out for me – I used to have very long hair in a ponytail, lovely golden blonde ponytail. Sister Thomas was telling me off and I went [flicked the hair back] *and she said, "Insolence. Go home, and don't come back until I've seen your mother". My poor mother was so upset. She had to go in, and she came home, and said, "You're having your hair cut off tomorrow morning. Sister Thomas says you're insolent and you've got to have it cut off". I was 13. That really hurt me.*

We used to do dressmaking, which was brilliant. I asked why we didn't do cookery, my sisters did that at Fulford, and they said, "We teach our girls to be career girls, not housewives". I liked games, I was right back at hockey, one of those filthy players, they didn't get by me. In some respects the Bar Convent was good for me, I had some lovely friends, I did meet a lot of people from different walks of life. They had ponies and I had a bike and it wasn't new. I think it stands you in good stead meeting different people later on in life.

Edna Scott aged 17, taken the week after leaving school. The first thing Edna did was to bleach her hair, with no-one to stop her now! (Edna Scott)

The art room was up the stairs, overlooking Nunnery Lane. And there was this hand in a little room on the way, [the hand of Margaret Clitherow]. *One person threw somebody's book from the top of the stairs to the bottom and Sister James looked straight at me. Nobody ever found out,* [who it was] *so we all got detention, which was a bit mean. None of us smoked but we decided we'd have a cigarette at lunchtime. It was quite a big hall and a big stage, and behind the curtains was stacked up scenery and furniture. We'd sneak behind the curtains and pass this Woodbine round. Because we didn't want anybody smelling it, we had a tin of baby talcum powder and we'd spray it round the back of the hall and it would be all white. We never got caught.*

I got suspended for my hair twice. I got suspended for so many bad conduct marks. You didn't have to do anything very untoward to get one. If you were seen without a beret outside school! The French teacher was about four foot six and she wore big high heels and bright red lipstick. She could shout for England. She used to come on the bus and we'd get off at the Rialto and you would try and get this hat on before the bus came. Ours were bright blue, I winged mine in the river as I left on the last day.

I got a Saturday job working at Woolworth's but as soon as they found out, Sister Thomas stopped that. My one bit of extra money. And my mother because she was so frightened of her, agreed. They were going round the class saying what did we want to do when we left. I said, "I want to be a hairdresser", they said, "That's not a career". One girl said, "I want to be an air hostess", (she was a boarder, used to fly back and forwards, her father worked in Kuwait). Sister Margaret Mary said, "You are not going to be an air hostess, that's a glorified bus conductress".

The only man was Mr Black, the piano teacher. The nuns used to be scurrying round. He must have thought he was the cream. I had a boyfriend and they used to come to the school at the side gate and all the girls would come and look at this boy and mates on motor bikes. How many bad conduct marks do you get for that? The kids now have a more relaxed life, it was black and white and nothing in between. When you have children of your own, you make damned sure they like the school they go to and make the most of everything. I did go to school with Sam Bartram's daughter, Moya. He was manager of York City. We were at school when the Manchester

Term ending .*12th April* .... 19 *33.*

Form *III Lower.* Number of Pupils in the Form.. *27* .. Position *18.*

REPORT ON THE WORK DONE.

SUBJECT	Term %	Exam %	REMARKS.
Religious Knowledge	48	49	Good
English Language and Literature	63	44	Capable of better work *K.C*
History	55	60	Fairly good but she makes little effort. *M.U.*
Latin			
French	22	21	Most unsatisfactory. E. is utterly lazy. *C.S*
Arithmetic	70	49	She is capable of better work. *M.U.*
Algebra			
Geometry			
Botany	65	53	Fairly good. She shows interest.
Physics			
Chemistry			
Geography	40	30	Unsatisfactory. She does not work *M.U.*
Drawing	50	70	Very good.
Needlework	100		Excellent *M.A*
Pianoforte			

Times late *10.* Times present *114.* out of a possible *121*

CONDUCT *Unsatisfactory*

PROGRESS *Unsatisfactory*

Signed *K Campion I B V M* Form Mistress
M. Aquinas IBVM Head Mistress

Next Term begins *Tuesday,*
Date *2nd May* 19 *33*

Signature of Parent or Guardian *A. Shearing.*
Date *2nd May* 19 *33.*

Anonymous report from Bar Convent 1933 (Mike Race)

United flight went down [in 1958, a flight from Munich crashed and some of the team were killed] *and she came into school with a black armband.*

I was good at maths. We had to stand on chairs and Sister Loyola used to go round each one, seven fours, eights sixes, like that. And if you got it wrong, you sat down. I always was the last man standing. That's my only claim to fame, that and my handwriting, I was proud of my certificate for winning the best handwriting in the North of England. I was about 12.

Thérèse Barton Rowan (née Healey) went to Bar Convent in 1973, having been to Our Lady's Primary School.

The 11 plus was just intelligence tests and we were schooled in them. We did it under exam conditions, so it wasn't frightening to go into this big silent hall and not be allowed to talk to anybody. It was a very useful skill.

Thérèse Healey, third from left on front row, at Bar Convent 1975, with teacher Ian Bentley
(Thérèse Barton Rowan)

You end up sorting people by ability at some stage in their lives. I saw people who came into the sixth form who'd been written off at 11, one went on to get a first in law at King's College, London. Every system works well for some people and not for others. If I'd failed my 11 plus and ended up in a school with kids who didn't want to work and who were causing chaos and bullying, I'd have been destroyed. I'd never have gone on and got a degree. Early segregation works well for academic people, but for people who are going to do well but not necessarily by the academic route, the 11 plus would have been a disaster.

I was extremely shy at school, and I just aimed not to be noticed and I think I did that quite successfully. I went through my whole school education thinking that I was nothing special. My highest point, apart from getting a degree later, was getting the form prize in Upper Fourth. I loved studying because I didn't particularly have any good friends, but in sixth form that all changed. The rules relaxed enormously and you were treated as individuals and independent. [At Bar Convent, the sixth form did not wear uniform, something which varied throughout the York sixth forms]. *And I made really good friends, so socially things worked very well for me. I was in junior choir for three years and senior the last four. And in Gallery Choir, a tiny choir that sang in chapel every morning.*

I quite liked games, but I was left handed which made me inconvenient for racket sports. So I would stand there getting cold and bored. But I did gym and swimming outside. And later on did the long jump and won it. When I went somewhere, I cartwheeled. I just liked to run and jump.

We had Miss Beckinsale for a while, the cousin of actor Richard Beckinsale. We thought she was fabulous because she was very young and used slightly dodgy language and was great fun. I liked English, I was sad that our teacher Mr Bentley died a year or two after I left, before I got an English degree. And I liked history with Mrs Smith. They were completely dedicated to their subjects and brought that over, they obviously loved to teach and put a lot of extra time and work in.

A tragedy occurred in the summer of Thérèse's final year, when Ian Smith, who had been physics master at Mill Mount from 1964 to 1970, then lecturer at York University, was charged with gassing his wife, Bar Convent teacher Margaret Smith aged 47. In 1981, the Yorkshire Evening Press reported the case. 'He attempted to make the death look like an accident, cycled nine miles from his home at Appleton Roebuck to the university to hide the carbon monoxide cylinders. He denied murder but admitted manslaughter on the grounds of diminished responsibility, and was jailed for three years'. He said he had marital problems and had decided to gas both her and himself but at the last minute could not go through with the suicide. The judge said, 'There are many times even in a normal marriage when a man wishes he could get rid of his wife, but I have to send you to prison because you killed a woman at the prime of her life'.

I remember the funeral at a little village church. Word hadn't yet come out that it was her husband. We were all completely devastated. But quite soon after, he was arrested. There wasn't much sympathy amongst my classmates I have to say. They said later he'd had some

Staff of Bar Convent 1975. Margaret Smith third from right, second row from front
(*Thérèse Barton Rowan*)

religious experience in prison and got out early for good behaviour. But we'd lost Mrs Smith.

We had a couple of days, like Mary Ward Day, when we got to do fun things all day, have stalls, do plays, watch movies. We put on Monty Python skits and did the 'Four Yorkshiremen' and had to borrow suits. We had the greatest fun. And someone streaked, at the time that streaking was quite common, she must have got money for charity.

There were lots of places you couldn't go. You couldn't walk down certain corridors or across the lovely little courtyard, you had to walk round. But I just loved going through the building. The boarders were completely separate. The sick bay was in the boarders' bit, you'd lay there and hear these distant noises of being in an ancient building. It was a beautiful building, we were very lucky. Decades later I looked back and thought how brilliant it had been, with these big windows, everywhere full of light. It had a beautiful library with wooden tables and book lined walls.

In our day you didn't question things. You got up in a morning and you went to school. So even if there was stuff you didn't like, you didn't make a fuss about it. I wouldn't have thought of questioning authority but you could do things to torture a teacher. You'd be sitting in a quiet room with 30 of you and she'd turn to the board and somebody would start to hum and she would turn round and that person would stop and somebody at the other side of the room would start. That kind of thing could just make the room completely unmanageable.

We knew there was absolutely no way she could control us if we chose to do something else. I'm not surprised that every school has people who have nervous breakdowns. It's a job where you can't relax. With any job if you're not having a great day and you cut some corners, you can get away with it, but teaching 14 year olds who don't want to be in school, you are never going to get away with anything. Being a good teacher isn't about being able to put the information across, having authority over a group of teenagers is probably the one vital thing. You could really see that with Mr Bentley. He did like being among developing minds. Why is it that one human being could walk in and you'd tear them to shreds and another would only have to put their head in and say, "What's happening here?", and you'd all be completely quiet? Maybe it's the confidence in their ability to do it.

I actually planned to be a nun and when we got to the Upper Sixth, me and two other girls got summoned to Sister James's office and she said, "You girls are the most likely to become nuns. My advice would be to go to college and then come back and join the order". And none of us became nuns.

Thérèse's sister, Bernadette Cass, started at the Convent two years earlier.

Bernadette Healey *(Bernadette Cass)*

It had a very good reputation. People wanted their children to go there. We did a lot of music and I really liked languages. Later I did a degree in Hispanic studies and psychology. It did reflect my interest in English, language and history. I played violin in the York Youth Orchestra at Queen Anne's on Saturday mornings. I was interested in singing and drama. We did lots of Shakespeare but also 16th century dramatists, Goldsmith and we did Bertolt Brecht, a whole range of things. And everyone could do something so people who didn't want to be on the stage could do lighting or costumes or make-up or the direction.

We did learn how not to be stressed about exams, and how to understand the questions and if you really couldn't do something, not to waste time but move on, which are pretty useful skills. We were stretched and I do wonder now how much education stretches pupils.

People aren't expected to attempt something that might be seen as difficult. If you don't have the experience of striving and either succeeding or not succeeding, then you don't learn about yourself and you don't know where your passions really are. We went to a school which valued academic performance very highly. There were people who got As in nearly everything and they were viewed as something special. And in games, if you were a naturally good tennis or netball player, the teachers would focus their time on that individual, because they were the ones with the aptitude that could get into competitions.

There were lots of rules about school uniform. There was a big fuss about the length of the skirt. We had some daring ones who took it up an inch or two and got sent home. Somebody came wearing platform shoes and she was suspended.

I've always been outspoken and that didn't always go down well. I wouldn't be pushed around at school so I ended up having conversations with Sister James because I wouldn't tolerate being told what to do without a reason. I don't remember any bullying. Sarcasm was the most vicious form that there was. Once I stormed out because I'd had a row with one of my friends. I got on the bus and went home. My poor mum said, "What on earth are you doing here?" And rang the school, who I don't think had noticed that I wasn't there. I remember Sister Thomas being incredibly nice. She had a very gentle exterior, and a core of steel. I always felt I could talk to her after that. She was a wonderful headmistress, she had communication skills, she could empathise.

I felt with hindsight, it was very sheltered. The conversations that we didn't have were quite telling, so there was never a conversation about what are you going to do with these A levels or this degree. The careers focus was helping you choose what university to apply to.

Getting an education was very important. It was expected that you would do the best you could. That was built in probably to our family background. When my dad talked about his education with monks [in Ireland], that was brutal, Today you wouldn't get away with it. They beat them, they humiliated them. There were some nice ones but if you were a teacher in that order, you could do anything to those children in your care. My dad had a great education and was happy with some of it but was unhappy with that behaviour. We were of a different culture 40 years later. It was a nice education, the values were good, the intent was good. To teach, you have to enjoy being with developing minds. You have to get something back from it, because if it's all about giving, it's just draining. There are people who are passionate about their subject, but are cut out to be academics or research scientists as opposed to being interested in young developing minds, who like the questions, don't mind the diversions, and get inspiration and energy from that.

CHAPTER 5

Single Sex
Secondary Modern Schools

York, like other cities in Britain, expanded quite dramatically into the suburbs during the 1930s, but building obviously stopped during the war. The 11 plus resulted in 20 per cent of pupils going to grammar schools, and by the late 1940s and 1950s there were a number of new secondary modern schools built around the city. Beckfield Lane School and Burnholme in Heworth were built in 1948, with Acomb Secondary Modern and Danesmead in Fulford built in 1954. Most of the schools were mixed, and only five were single sex – Park Grove School, St George's and York Model School for Boys, Burton Stone Lane and Knavesmire for girls.

ST GEORGE'S SECONDARY MODERN SCHOOL

St George's Junior School opened a separate higher grade department in 1928, but in 1936 a new boys' secondary school was built on land in George Street off Walmgate. It was used as a store for Rowntree's factory during the war and not officially opened until 1948. It was largely built for the Catholic community in the area, though boys from further afield also attended.

Mike Race joined the school in 1949.

The education we received at the junior school was very poor. An aging teacher who taught the older children was often away ill and her replacements, including a lady from Bermuda who struggled to hold our attention, had little knowledge of preparing children for the 11 plus. Only one child from the 40 or so who took the exam in my year, actually passed (although I believe four or five later transferred

Mike Race 1949 *(Mike Race)*

to grammar schools, including one boy called Reggie Wood who eventually won a scholarship to an elite American University). The rest were 'condemned' to a secondary modern education.

There wasn't a Catholic grammar school in the city, you had to go to Leeds to St Michael's. I was one of those who failed but was later interviewed with a view to a possible transfer to Nunthorpe, but, partly through intimidation by a boorish panel member, I failed again, which was probably just as well. I might have struggled, and although my parents were disappointed, I was rather relieved, as it meant I could stay with my friends at St George's.

Before starting we were given a list of requirements. One of these was a towel for use after PE. My mother saw it as a duty to preserve the modesty of her only child by also supplying swimming trunks, and both being 'innocents abroad', this seemed right to me. After the first lesson, and being slow to undress, I saw, to my horror, the other boys dashing into the showers naked. I hastily hid my trunks amongst my clothes before taking a deep breath and joining them.

We were taught by three brothers of the De La Salle order, Brother Matthew, Brother Vincent and Brother Ilted, plus the headmaster Brother Baptist, and six lay teachers including Mr Campbell, the deputy head. I thought the teachers strict. Mr Brophy, an ex-army officer, lined the boys up outside his classroom and checked for clean hands and polished shoes and the cane would follow if warnings about cleanliness hadn't been addressed.

Most of the teachers used the cane, and on one memorable occasion Brother Vincent caned the whole class during a maths lesson when they were unable to understand the question. Brother Ilted, the PE teacher, also had a reputation for frequent use of the cane, but as I rarely attended PE, this is hearsay! I once got four of the best from

Brother Baptist and I remember him saying, "This is going to hurt me more than it's going to hurt you". However I don't believe the teachers were violent bullies. Corporal punishment was the rule, and I don't think the boys harboured any resentment over its use. The teachers were competent rather than outstanding. The lessons by Mr Burns the science teacher were looked forward to as he would often use practical and exciting demonstrations in his class. He was the only teacher with a degree. He had a cannon on his desk and would shoot chalk at pupils who were misbehaving. If you turned to talk to someone, the chalk would hit you on the back of the head. He never missed. Brother Vincent was a good teacher, he taught art and maths and excelled in writing script. He hand-scripted a missal that was sent to the Vatican and is still used for the mass there. He also held debates and ran the chess club, a game in which the school excelled, winning the York Chess League on at least one occasion in the 1950s and being near the top in most years. I remember going to Mill Mount and playing, and we did postal chess with other schools.

St George's Chess Club 1950 (Mike Race)

Joe Campbell was an English teacher, one of the old school, usually dressed in a three piece tweed suit, with a pipe in his mouth. Most of his lessons seemed to consist of boys reading aloud. 'Lorna Doone' seemed to occupy one year and 'The Merchant of Venice' another. Mr Smithers the metalwork teacher was a fine pianist and I believe composed the school song, 'Years of sturdy toil have formed us, men have fought with valiant hearts, in their love for old St George's, now we sing, "We'll do our part".'

Mr Barker, the history teacher, once caught some of the boys swimming in the River Foss in the nude, with girls from St Wilfrid's. They were paraded in front of the school in assembly and then marched to be paraded at St Wilfrid's.

The school placed a strong emphasis on practical subjects. You were being schooled for jobs which were physical, factory based, or apprenticeships. Some people did become teachers. They must have taken further education when they left school. It had a reputation as a rough school, but although I was certainly no 'tough guy' I wasn't aware of a bullying culture. There were occasional fights but they were the exception rather than the rule, and the smaller, weaker element didn't seem to be picked on unduly.

It was a small school with no more than 320 pupils in eight classes. The main classrooms were on two storeys, and ran parallel with Margaret Street. The school was corridored, all glass. It had two wings, one contained the hall, and one contained the gym, above were metalwork

St George's School 1953 (Mike Race)

111

St George's Football Team 1953. Mike Race far left on back row, third from right is Phil Scott (York Archaeological Trust staff in 1990s) (Mike Race)

and woodwork rooms, and a playground in the middle. The woodwork room looked onto Walmgate lodging houses. You could see the itinerant workers there, mostly Irish, wandering about in just their shirts. I hated woodwork and metalwork so it was more interesting to look out and see what was going on.

It was very close to St George's Church. I was an altar boy and sometimes during the day the priest would come for two of us to participate in funerals. We'd get 2/6d to share. I did try my best and was usually near the top of the class and I was a keen Catholic. They tried to integrate this element of competition. One of the things was how much money you would give for masses for the dead. It was on a graph on the board. I was in De La Salle house. My mother once gave half a crown, so that put our house way above the others. I was quite popular with the Brothers because of that.

The school always had a reputation for having the best school rugby league team in York. I was good at sport. We were in leagues on Saturday mornings for football and we played cricket at Fenby Field. We won the John Lund cricket trophy, the first time I'd ever won anything, I was 14. But I hated PE and with another friend, Terry, we decided we wouldn't go, we just used to walk out. I remember walking down the street and one of the teachers came along, said, "Hello", and walked on. But nothing happened. I wondered later if the teacher might have thought I had been at a funeral. Perhaps the reason I avoided it was because I'd heard if you couldn't vault over the horse, you would get hit with a slipper.

School dinners cost fourpence and weren't very good. I always got stuck with kids who were throwing food about, which was irritating. Friday was an awful day, it would be some horrible fish, with turnips and lumpy potatoes, then tapioca or semolina. Sometimes we'd go down town to the Petergate fish shop to get a scallop, a potato in batter with a bit of fish, and some chips. That came to threepence. Then we'd get a bag of broken biscuits for a penny. It was far more satisfying than school meals. There were little corner shops close to school, you could pop out to buy liquorice, the nearest thing to a school tuck shop.

We had St Patrick's concerts, which were very good fun. They were held every year at the Rialto, probably because Mr Prendergast was a Catholic, and were very well attended. I remember one year we marched as soldiers to 'They're

St Patrick's Day concert 1949. Mike Race is second from left in middle row (Mike Race)

Changing Guard at Buckingham Palace'. I was 12 or 13. There was singing, and gymnastic displays and a group dressed up for a musical piece. But the highlight was the club swinging. The place was darkened and they used two wooden illuminated clubs and swung them in time to the music.

I think the 11 plus is a very crude general way of selecting people. It's no point giving everybody a wonderful education and saying,

"You can now be an archaeologist or a teacher", when they haven't got the ability to do so. You need people who are going to work in Macdonald's, sweep the roads, pack chocolates. It was chosen so that the people who had the ability got the best education. You need to have that to work in a certain strata in society. A lot of people must now be educated beyond their ability yet a lot seem to leave school not being able to read and write. Some people are more intelligent than others, and will get on no matter what. Captain James Cook was born in poor circumstances and finished up by being one of the world's greatest navigators, because he'd got that drive within him. If you've got it, you will succeed, and others who are bright need that extra push to take them forward. There are others who can be pushed until you are blue in the face and they will never become anything other than mediocre in terms of education.

St George's School before demolition, at top of Margaret Street (Mike Race)

I came out being able to read and write to a reasonably good standard. I had a pretty good basic knowledge of history and geography, I knew a lot about Catholicism. In terms of how to behave socially, we seemed to have respect for teachers. I don't remember any careers people coming round, but about 50 per cent of the boys said they wanted to be motor mechanics. I got an apprenticeship and went to Ben Johnson's. The beauty of Rowntree's, Terry's and the railway, was that boys who left education with nothing, in terms of GCEs, had the opportunity to develop within the company. I finished up as a manager through time.

St George's closed in the 1970s and was demolished in 1996, making way for flats.

THE YORK MODEL SCHOOL/ ST JOHN'S SECONDARY MODERN SCHOOL

This school opened in 1859 as a demonstration school with 80 boys, the Model School for York and Ripon Diocesan Training College in Lord Mayor's Walk, later St John's College. Its entrance was in the Groves. In 1900, it was designated an elementary school but had fees and a special status. In 1910 there were 193 boys. In 1932 the Model School became a senior boys' school, and after 1948 continued as a voluntary aided secondary modern school for boys, with 200 pupils in 1956. The school was run as a department of the college until 1963 when it became a separate building.

John Lightfoot attended the school from 1963 until its closure in 1965.

The headmaster was Mr Hobbs, Mr Green taught science and technical drawing. Mr [Graham] McLennan started a school boxing team and I had two boxing matches for the school. I won the first match but lost the second on account of being out reached by my opponent. On a school day trip to Whitby in 1965, on a dull and misty day, I took some photos with my Kodak

St John's School trip to Whitby 1965, with teachers John Langton and Victor Green (John Lightfoot)

John Lightfoot on St John's School trip to Whitby 1965 (John Lightfoot)

Brownie box camera, including my great teacher of history, maths, art and classical music, John Langton, with Victor Green (a nice genial man).

Ken Humphreys, who later taught at Manor, recalls teaching at the Model School.

It was small in number, a smashing staff, really strong men teachers. I remember Mr McLennan, who had come over from New Zealand, to play for York Rugby League Club. [He went on to teach at Knavesmire and was President of York Schools Athletic Association in 1982]. *And a very strong character, Harry Butcher, I think he played football in York. One year, the school was awarded the Brian Woodcock trophy which went generally to individuals, but on this occasion it was the whole school, for sporting prowess throughout the year.*

KNAVESMIRE SECONDARY SCHOOL FOR GIRLS

Knavesmire Council School opened in April 1916, and became one of York's higher grade schools, with accommodation for boys, girls and infants. With the introduction of the tripartite system, the school split into a primary school and secondary school for girls.

Heather Norton (née Page) and Jean Leeman (née Thompson) were both born in 1938, met at Knavesmire and remain close friends. Heather came from Scotland.

I was different because of my accent. Miss Spence, the headmistress, at Robbie Burns' time, made me get up on the stage and recite 'A

Aerial view of Knavesmire School 1960s (Lynne Townend)

puddock sat by the lochan's brim', so I really felt Scottish. I got sick of people asking, "Could you repeat that?" I was never bullied, it was all in very good humour. I just got used to being with the girls so [eventually] I talked like them.

It was a very happy school. They were caring. Pam was another of our friends. In that first year her father died tragically and the teacher said it would be nice if we all looked after her.

I loved history particularly. I came from a village outside Glasgow so York to me was wonderful. We had Miss Wright as a history teacher. We used to go to the Castle Museum sometimes for lessons.

We came just after the war. A lot of the teachers were in the war, so the older ladies came out of retirement. We had the end of the retirees and the younger women and men coming into the profession.

Class 1950. Back row fifth from left – Jean Thompson, Heather Page second from left on second row from back (Heather Norton)

Jean recalls that the school had a flat above it, which the girls had to clean as part of their domestic science lessons. This was a new innovation in the 1950s.

> *It did give you an insight into how to go on in a home of your own. You had to polish the floor. I found a new way, by putting two dusters underneath the coconut mat and pushing myself around on my bum. Unfortunately I was discovered doing that so I had to polish it twice. In cookery I once went home with a stewed saddlebag, it was supposed to be in a jam jar but the lid had come off. My father was looking forward to this Knavesmire School stew but I'm afraid it was thrown in the bin because it was swimming in my saddle bag.*

Heather remembers the flat.

> *You cleaned cupboards out and made sure everything was neat, you did shopping lists as well. If tins had disappeared, you had to replenish the shelves. You learnt how to make the bed and hoover the*

carpets. And we made our aprons and headbands for cookery out of
calico.

The girls played hockey, netball, rounders and cricket. Heather

*loved rounders. Knavesmire was well known for having a very good
team. I can remember my father taking me onto the Knavesmire and
throwing a hard ball at me to get my fingers nimble. Joan Rowland,
the PE teacher, did Scottish country dancing after school, and I
enjoyed that a lot. She used to go to the country dance class in the
Merchant Taylor's where I went with my mother.*

*I used to cycle to Dringhouses for piano lessons. My aunt was
the pianist for the Glasgow Orpheus Choir, and when Sir Hugh
Robertson was away during the war, she'd take the choir. And then
years later she had choirs of her own in Scotland.*

*Class 1953 with Miss Polly Kettlewell. Heather Page second from left on back row, Jean Thompson
fourth from right (Heather Norton)*

Jean recalls science.

I vividly remember being in the lab and Mrs Rowland passing the sheep's bladder round with a glass tube stuck in one end. Everybody had to blow down it and watch the bladder blow up. It got to my turn, she said, "Don't forget, you must blow not suck", and

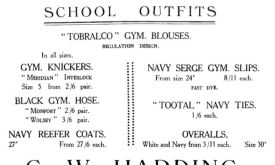

SCHOOL OUTFITS

"TOBRALCO" GYM. BLOUSES.
REGULATION DESIGN.
In all sizes.

GYM. KNICKERS.
" MERIDIAN " INTERLOCK
Size 5 from 2/6 pair.

BLACK GYM. HOSE.
" MONFORT " 2/6 pair.
" WOLSEY " 3/6 pair.

NAVY REEFER COATS.
27″   From 27/6 each.

NAVY SERGE GYM. SLIPS.
From size 24″   8/11 each.
FAST DYE.

" TOOTAL " NAVY TIES.
1/6 each.

OVERALLS.
White and Navy from 3/11 each.   Size 30″

G. W. HARDING

High Ousegate and Coppergate

Tel. 2550.   York.

that was it, I just couldn't do it. I was thinking of what was inside the damn thing. It was revolting.

I remember [one of the teachers] *losing her knickers coming into the classroom. I think the elastic gave way at the waist so they dropped down, the legs remained in situ. She took two or three steps into the room, lost her drawers and hastily reversed out. But you didn't laugh. It was never talked about with the teachers. We had one teacher and she would wear interlock knickers, like thick flannelette. They were called harvest festivals, they had elastic, 'all safely gathered in'. One of the girls used to be always dropping a pencil on the floor, have a geg along the row and then come up and say, 'Blue today'.*

Heather admits

We were always in trouble for talking. If there was any noise, it would be our group at the back. We'd get lines or go to see Miss Spence in her room. And you'd wait for nearly half an hour outside and then go in and get a lecture. One of the other things was to be sent out into the corridor, which wasn't really a punishment. Our rooms faced the playground and whenever people were playing games, we'd daydream, watching out of the window. So we'd get sent out.

You've got to respect the teacher. If you knew you had to be quiet and get on with your books and listen to the lesson, you did so. If they were quietly spoken, and had no command of the class, it's gone.

Jean recalls there were more severe punishments at junior school.

They used the cane at Scarcroft. One of the lads had his hand hit so hard that the cane split, it was such a mess, there was blood all over. There was quite a row about that. I never liked the fellow that did this, he'd been in the war and was a bit brutal and he hit his hand far too hard. It was only something childish when all is said and done.

Later, the older girls would help at Knavesmire Infants' School next door, and Heather recalls

We went over at lunchtimes and put them to sleep on little beds. We'd tuck them in and look after them.

Heather feels that children were more innocent at that time.

I'd never worn a pair of stockings, up to 15 you were still children. You went out and played cricket with the boys and rounders on the Knavesmire. The kids now, they're having babies at the most ridiculous age. It was a different life then, a happier life. We were disciplined, we knew right from wrong. I think they've lost a lot of their childhood and the great things that we had, we had no worries. You went out and ran around with the boys. It was only a laugh and a giggle.

We did our homework and then you could go out and play. Play was a great part of your life. You had to be in by eight o'clock and you were in trouble if you weren't home at the right time. Now you see kids at ten o'clock at night, sitting on a pavement. Or they're on the computer for hours on end. It's not as healthy.

Jean recalls a character from school who was

a little tea leaf. She'd pinch anything. If anything went missing, she'd have it. We'd lift her desk lid and have a look in. I don't think the teachers were on to her. We just dealt with it ourselves.

The ink monitor was a great job to have for a term. I was the ink monitor once, I used to test the depth of the inkwell with Pam's plaits. We had a big bottle and would fill them up.

Heather was the milk monitor.

You had to put your hands up every night if you wanted milk next day. It was a luxury after the war, something that the government did.

Jean recalls,

In winter it was rising up out of the bottle with the lid sat on the top, you had to put it on the radiator. It was still horrible.

We wore gymslips, blue blouses, [prefects wore white], tie, blazer, beret and white socks. But some had school uniform and some hadn't. I was always aware that those who hadn't, couldn't afford them.

Heather took a pride in her satchel.

We polished them, they were lovely leather. And your leather shoes were always polished to the highest. My dad used to do them each night. It kept the rain out.

Jean has also been a guide in York. She has always loved history and art.

I went into a drawing office, so I do neat, smallish drawings. Most of the paintings I've done are of York. School was your training for the future. I think we learned quite a lot, even if it was only about the cotton boll weevil.

Heather believes that school

gives you a basic grounding. When you go on holidays, you have a rough idea of where it is on the map. I think history has played a great part in my life, and latterly after I'd had the children, maths.

We lived life to the full. I tried to do as much as I could. To me you have a childhood, then an adult and then a family life.

Janet Pigott (née Taylor) joined Knavesmire in 1950. She attended three different junior schools, with Scarcroft as the final one.

Janet Taylor and mother Violet 1943 (Janet Pigott)

When I was 10 in 1949, I developed a serious infection, alleged to have been from my frequent swimming, and was admitted to the County Hospital. Mum and Dad were bothered about my loss of schooling because the scholarship exams were approaching.

Mum went to see the headmistress and asked if I could be given some homework but she refused. She said her staff had enough to do in the daytime without having to mark homework as well. Mum and Dad were disappointed with her attitude and gave me some books to read. I loved Enid Blyton and read all her Famous Five books.

I sat the scholarship but had never seen anything like it before. We were given a booklet containing 100 questions based on shapes and had to write down which shape was the odd one out. I rushed through the booklet, just putting down any numbers, then went back to the beginning and looked more carefully. It was a useless task, and I couldn't see any value in it. I was only about a third of the

Prefect Badge *(York City Archives)*

way through the second perusal when the teacher said, "Stop". Needless to say I chose to go to Knavesmire. On the first day, we were greeted at the door by what I thought were enormously tall girls with 'Prefect' badges.

We were welcomed by Miss Spence, the headmistress. I was allocated to form 1A. My teacher was Mrs B A Ferguson, BA. Some of the girls asked why she had her initials at the end of her name as well as the beginning. She told us her name was Bertha Agatha Ferguson, and the BA at the end meant she had a Bachelor of Arts, she had been to university. She had a daughter, Elspeth, [at Mill Mount] who was a member of York City Swimming and trained under Lonz Webster. My parents had made me give up swimming lessons after my hospital treatment so I was always interested to hear of Elspeth's progress. In 1956 she was a trialist for the Melbourne Olympics. She came fourth in the eighth qualifying round, and was more successful in the European championships in Hungary.

We had a house system based on the names of abbeys in Yorkshire. Girls allotted to Byland wore blue sashes, mine was yellow because I was in Fountains, those in Rievaulx wore red, and Jervaulx house wore green. Once a year we would have house competitions, in the form of sports events in the playground, hockey on the Knavesmire, and swimming in Rowntree's Park baths.

There was an achievement chart on the wall. We were allocated different coloured stars, the highest being gold. Black stars were for bad behaviour, lack of effort and truancy. One black star cancelled out three good ones. For really bad behaviour, the teacher had a cane. A miscreant would have to stand at the front of the class and hold her hand out. Sometimes, in a natural reaction, a girl would withdraw her hand before the cane landed on it. Then she had to put out both hands and take the punishment twice over.

A girl called Ann Atkinson was a talented pianist and when we had Musical Appreciation lessons with Miss McKenzie, they used to play duets together. My favourite was the Arrival of the Queen of Sheba. I begged my parents to buy a piano. They bought an ancient thing with yellowed keys and fretwork legs but I thought it was wonderful. They found an elderly piano teacher, Mr Horner in Bewlay Street, and once a week I would go with my Hermann's Fingering Exercise book and 1s 3d to pay for an hour's lesson.

My parents didn't go out socialising but they did take me and Keith [her brother] *to the bonfire on Scarcroft Green. Once someone let off a jumping cracker near us. It touched my leg at the back of my heel and burnt a small hole in my navy blue lisle stocking. Next morning the hole had become much bigger. I got fed up with people telling me that they could see my white flesh so I dipped my finger in the inkwell and painted my skin through the hole. That night Grandma darned it with navy blue wool.*

In 1952 the headmistress recommended that I tried for the 13 plus exam for late entry to a grammar school [taken at Mill Mount]. *But once again I failed. Instead of concentrating on what I was doing, and getting on with writing an essay, I gazed out of the window at pupils playing tennis below. I was entranced with their efforts and dreamed of the day when I'd be joining them, but I hadn't worked hard enough to warrant a pass. I was disappointed, but my Mum and Dad were even more upset. At least I was happy in my school and it was better for me to be at the top end of my class at Knavesmire, than bottom at Mill Mount. To combat my disappointment, I got more and more involved with the Girl Guides.*

The Queen's coronation in 1953 was a major event. At school we were given a coronation mug and a New Testament to commemorate the event. Later the school went to see a film about it.

Nellie Buckley, Janet Taylor and Diana York in Girl Guides 1955
(Janet Pigott)

Our fourth form teacher was a doddery elderly lady called Miss Kettlewell. All the pupils called her 'Polly put the kettle on'. I was not impressed with her spelling. When I was in the third year, she told me I'd spelt water wrongly. "You've missed an R out". I told her that there was only one R in water. Other pupils joined in and eventually she got a dictionary. She apologised and said she must have spelt it wrong all her life! It wasn't the first spelling mistake she'd made. I remember her putting the word banana on the blackboard and spelling it with a double n!

During PE, I used to slope off into the library. Only once was I ever caught, by Miss Brown, the needlework teacher. I told her that I was the library monitor and had to count the history books. She believed me and I continued to evade PE throughout the rest of my schooldays. When my parents got my school report at the end of every term, for PE Miss Boynton had always written 'fair'!

My favourite teacher was Miss Harper who taught domestic science. At first we learnt about housework, cleaning, washing a blouse and ironing all the double parts, then baking jam tarts, sausage rolls, and cakes. In our third year she taught us cake decorating. I took to the skill like a duck to water. We practised by skimming an upturned cake tin with lard. It was much cheaper than using icing sugar. Often the heat of our fingers would turn it to oil, but we practised until we were perfect. By the fourth year, we were ready to use genuine ingredients. We took a rich fruit cake and had to pay for ground almonds, eggs and icing sugar. I made a basket of roses. Mum and Dad couldn't believe I'd done it myself. To prove it, I did another one at home, moulding the roses from marzipan, and colouring them with pink and yellow. I bought some artificial fern frond from Border's in Coney Street, and wove the icing in and out in basket weave. They were amazed and invited all the neighbours in to show it off.

Most subjects weren't very challenging. Mrs Ferguson ran a leisure hour competition and Dad suggested that I made him a saddle bag. He got a piece of thick canvas and we folded it over to make the right shape, with a flap for the lid. Sewing the leather straps on was very hard. He bought some saddlery needles which were curved, and thick beeswax-impregnated thread. My efforts were 'Highly Commended' and I was awarded a prize, the book 'A Short History of York' by Marguerita Spence, my headmistress. I was very proud and pleased to have it. It was the first thing I'd ever won.

In 1954 I sat the entrance test to attend York City Technical College in Clifford Street, and passed. By the time I left I was walking tall, and developed a new self confidence that I'd never known before. I was at Technical College for two and a half years and left with four O levels and eight RSA secretarial qualifications.

Janet always felt she was not good enough because she failed the 11 plus but after getting her qualifications, she became a secretary. She met her husband when he was a student teacher, and they moved to Essex. One of his colleagues taught at an evening institute and they required a shorthand teacher. Janet applied, and went on to study via correspondence and then work at a private school. By 1972 she was lecturing in secretarial skills and in 1978 did the B Ed course. She wrote a manual on word processing, used widely for many years, ran a Diploma in word processing and set up a Chamber of Commerce and Industry Private Secretary's Diploma course which was very successful.

Lynne Townend (née Reed) went to

Knavesmire in 1962. I remember the night before getting things ready. I can even smell the new leather satchel. I remember having new pens, and backing the books with patterned paper. I think it was the newness of it, it was exciting.

I wanted to go to an all girls' school, thinking it would be really nice. It wasn't as nice as it was made out to be. I was bullied. On my report a teacher had written, 'Lynne has been somewhat unhappy this term'. And I was dreading my mum and dad saying something. In those days you just got on with it. But they just signed it, and I was really relieved. It was psychological type abuse, it wasn't physical. It was just one or two people. If you're not confident and you're a bit insecure, you can lay yourself open to things like that. But that got better when we moved to the new school.

Knavesmire Choir, Lynne Reed third from right on middle row. 1964 (Lynne Townend)

In 1964, Knavesmire School moved to Middlethorpe.

They needed a bigger school. The population was growing. They got boys in my third year, about 1965, the first intake was in the first year. They had to start and work their way through.

Lynne recalls the school flat.

It was for the fifth form, and I never went into it, it was where girls could learn to be wives and mothers. It changed because of modern thinking that women don't have to stay and look after the house. They could work. They were also accommodating a lot more subjects. I liked history more than anything. I did a project on the River Ouse, and York Minster and I did a project on New Earswick and how that village came about. I did struggle with maths and science and those teachers gave me a lot of support. Later we did civics, about local government and law, how the country relates to us.

I was in the choir all the way through. I did enjoy that. The school song, I think it was 'And did those feet in ancient times', Jerusalem. In my last year we got Mr Marshall who taught English and drama. He was charismatic. Suddenly someone coming in, younger with new ideas, it was like 'wow'. A girl got a photo of him and she was selling them, because we all had a crush on him.

We did a play and had to dress really simply and had to wear masks to convey our character. That was very modern. I really did enjoy it. I have a feeling I was King Herod. I remember, 'Herod am I, the king of Israel and Judah, and the

English teacher Clive Marshall, centre on front row 1966
(Lynne Townend)

Drama 1965, Lynne Reed second from left (Lynne Townend)

mightiest conqueror that walked this earth'. We had speech days where people got prizes for achievement, I've still got mine. A poetry book, for work in English.

We used to put on records at lunchtime and mime to them. We had a girl called Norma who sang some John Lennon songs and she could look like him, and Sandie Shaw.

But I thought school was a bit dull. School is school, you just have to go and get home again. They weren't the best time of my life. It was a necessity one has to go through. Being bullied initially always made me aware of that. It made me unhappy at the time, but it wasn't intense. When my kids went to school, I wanted to know what it was like, what went on. My mum and dad would never have asked me that. I didn't blame them, that was the way it was.

Despite early difficulties, Lynne blossomed in the last two years. Often an inspiring teacher can make all the difference. Her report read, 'You have an enquiring mind, individual personality and individuality of thought'.

When we went into the fifth form it was a much smaller group. You developed closer relationships because there weren't so many of you. It was more intimate.

The school closed in 1985 and was bought by the new College of Law in 1988.

Reunion of Class of 1967 in 1999. Lynne Townend standing far right on second row (Lynne Townend)

BURTON STONE LANE SCHOOL FOR GIRLS

This school was built in 1939 in Evelyn Crescent, on the Water Lane estate, and initially called Water Lane School. It opened in October 1942 and girls from Shipton Street were transferred there. There was accommodation for 320 but there were only 104. The building was extended in 1945, and by 1956 there were 560 pupils. The school closed in August 1985.

Joyce Botham (née Wilson) started with her twin sister Julie in 1967.

My dad always wanted us to go to an all girls' school. He was hoping we'd pass the 11 plus and go to a grammar school. So when Christine [her elder sister] *didn't, he decided she would go to Burton Stone, because it was the only all girls' secondary*

Julie, Joyce and Christine Wilson 1969 (Joyce Botham)

131

modern and I enjoyed it but felt frustrated a lot of the time, there was no opportunity to do a lot of the subjects that I wanted to do.

Most people were doing CSEs, only a few girls did GCE. And even that was a fight. I wanted to do Art GCE and the school weren't prepared to run a course just for me. Mum and Dad had to kick up a fuss, and agree to pay the entrance fee for the examination. The art teacher, Mrs Cox, said, "I'm prepared to do extra work with her. The art room will be available whenever she wants to come in".

I've never done physics, chemistry, Latin, or the traditional grammar school subjects because they weren't on offer.

Despite this, Joyce found the particular advantage of Burton Stone was the

family pastoral atmosphere. There was a lot of social life, they put fashion shows on, a disco every Friday. There was a lot of netball and sport which I enjoyed, but a lot of emphasis on needlework. They assumed that girls that went to secondary modern schools, all they had to aspire to was being wives and mothers. There was a domestic science block, two rooms fully equipped, beautiful. There was a flat with bedrooms and a little kitchen and girls were taught how to look after the house, how to iron, starch collars, to darn, and a lot of emphasis on cookery. We were shown how to make bread, every year we made a Christmas cake, it was a big production, it would take you weeks.

While I was at school my mum went to mature student college and became a teacher. I got a little bit more confident. I was doing quite well so I decided to try for sixth form. You had to have at least three GCEs for Mill Mount to even consider you. I passed English language, domestic science and art, and got in. In the November I did some re-sits, I got more qualifications in the two years at the grammar school, five more O levels plus an A level, because that environment suited me. I felt I was where I should have been.

Mill Mount was very exam-related. I was quite happy that I was holding my own academically. There wasn't that close relationship between teacher and pupil that there was at the secondary modern. I never felt as if I fitted in socially. A lot of girls in the sixth form had been with each other for years. It was the first time I'd been on my own. Everywhere else I'd been I always had Julie. Julie went to nursing college, so it was very different lives all of a sudden.

The relationship with the art teacher at Mill Mount was super. I had big gaps in my knowledge of art history and my skill base so the teacher, Mrs Jewels, took me under her wing and used to give me extra sessions.

Mill Mount Garden Party 1975, staff dress as pupils (Joyce Botham)

You were very much left to independent learning and were expected to be self motivated. At Burton Stone, there were people motivating you, checking that you'd done your work. At the grammar school, not as much teaching went on, as reliance on textbooks. The day that we left Burton Stone, my dad came to school with a big bunch of flowers. There were tears, teachers hugging you and wishing you well.

I walked away from Mill Mount and I don't think anybody as much as said cheerio. Apart from the leaving assembly which was more to inspire you to go on and do greater things. There was no warmth at Mill Mount. Burton Stone was a nurturing environment. It was an academic environment at Mill Mount.

Joyce Wilson (now Botham) on far left, skipping 1970s *(Joyce Botham)*

But I was a girl on a mission. I wanted the academic bit. I'd had the nurturing. I felt quite nurtured and safe in the school environment, which is probably why I've never left it. School has always been a brilliant place. I've loved it right from being five and I've got my own school now.

When I was about 30, I sat the mature entrance exam and started the four year honours degree at St John's in applied linguistics and social sciences. It was really hard work, I had two little boys and a home and a husband. I did my degree then a one year post grad teaching certificate course. Later a Master's in Educational Research and then the qualification for Headship at Teesside University.

Joyce is now head teacher at Sutton on the Forest Primary School and does consultancy work for the local authority.

It's very fulfilling, I love it and I'm surrounded by kids all day.

Joyce feels that the seeds which led to her current position were sown at Burton Stone.

And it must be something to do with perseverance. A lot of things have happened, that could have knocked me back. Julie died while I was doing my finals. Because I've got a strong family background and I've always had this drive, it's been the saving grace.

Academic life kept me going. I could lose myself in books. And meeting Steve [her husband] *gave me the confidence in myself. When I got my degree in the Minster, it was less than a year after Julie died. That was very moving.*

I've always enjoyed the challenge of reaching for things that I couldn't get. If it had all been there on a plate, I might not have had the aspirations that I had. We were made to feel special at Burton Stone. Not in an academic way, that was never a high priority. It was more your personality and the life skills that you needed. The academic side came from Mill Mount. What I am as a person came from Burton Stone.

Burton Stone Community Centre 2010. (Part of site was Burton Stone School) (Oliver Bostock)

– CHAPTER 6 –

Mixed Secondary Modern Schools

By the 1960s, York had 15 mixed secondary modern schools. These were Acomb, Ashfield, Beckfield, Danesmead, Derwent, Lowfield, St Margaret Clitherow, Park Grove and St Wilfrid's which no longer exist, plus Burnholme, Canon Lee, Fulford, Huntington, Joseph Rowntree and Manor, which became comprehensive schools.

ASHFIELD

In 1897 the Ashfield Estate on Tadcaster Road was bought for £15,000 by Edward Lycett Green, second baronet. His father Sir Edward owned Nunthorpe Hall, and his brother Frank took over the Treasurer's House, which he restored and gave to the National Trust in 1930. After Edward died in 1940 aged 79, the war department took over the Ashfield estate, which was bought by York City Council in 1948, becoming a secondary modern school in 1957.

Ashfield School badge
(Michael Sargent)

Michael Sargent was born in 1938 in Derbyshire, and educated at Chesterfield Grammar School. He trained as a teacher at St Luke's College, Exeter.

> *If you were to read the press reports about the opening of Ashfield, 'There are facilities for training the future housewives of the day with home economics…and the future mechanics of the day',*
> *it didn't become like that, it was right across the board and we catered for all abilities.* [70 boys from Scarcroft Secondary School had moved there at Easter 1957 and they took the first intake of

Michael Sargent's 5th form class 1960s (Michael Sargent)

girls in September]. *By the time I arrived in 1960, it was vastly
overcrowded. It had been built for 480 pupils and there were 720. In
1962, some people were given the chance of staying to do O levels.
We were one of the first secondary moderns to do that. By that time,
numbers had reduced because Lowfield School had been built and of
the first years, half of them transferred there.*

*The head was a man called Mr Joe Turner, who had been head at
Scarcroft. He was a good teacher but the disciplinarian was the
deputy head,* [also from Scarcroft], *Mr* [Clement] *Tubman. Children
used to say they were frightened of him. I remember saying, "Don't
worry because we are frightened of him too". He kept the school in
order.*

*I could never say Ashfield was a typical secondary modern. They drew
largely from a good catchment area and the majority of parents were
very supportive and we did try to bring the best out of the youngsters.
Some people did extremely well because they were not in competition
with people who had been deemed brighter at 11. Those in the A*

Cricket team 1960s, Michael Sargent far right (Michael Sargent)

stream would probably have been in the C stream at a grammar school.

At one time there were 16 members of staff of which only two were ladies, then it began to even itself out. We had a men's staffroom and a women's staffroom until we got a new headmaster in 1969 and one of the first things he did was to have a joint one.

I taught maths and RE. I did quite a lot on the games field as well, looked after the soccer and cricket teams. We were a young staff, got on well socially and quite a number were interested in sport. You had a form and that gave you the chance to know youngsters very well. One particular class are in their 50th year now and we still see a lot of each other. It's good that they can accept their former teacher has become a friend.

A number took the 13 plus, some went on to a grammar school, and talking to parents, they said they regretted that, because they had been the cream at Ashfield and became the skimmed milk at grammar school. By 1966 we had half the fourth year staying on to do O level or CSE and we got some good results. One person [Rachel Parker] *went to Ashfield, transferred to Mill Mount and won an open exhibition to Oxford. The headline in the paper was '11 plus failure gets Oxford place'. She said, "Ashfield was where I got the grounding". That was a feather in Ashfield's cap.*

Discipline was very good. Corporal punishment was used sparingly, but as a deterrent. There are people who remind me I once gave them the slipper or cane but they said, "We deserved it". It was used if a person was caught smoking or if there'd been instances of bullying or acts of stupidity, like throwing a rubber across the room. The building was never damaged, graffiti wasn't on the walls, there were people walking round school all the time and they were being noted.

Back Row: John Gargett, Trevor Clark, Alan Ashton, Geoffrey Medd, Dave Jeffries, Geoffrey Lowson, John Butler, Raymond Wood, Alan Mortimer, Barry Hodgson, Barry Fowler, Billy Hulme, James Lockhart

Front Row: John Stather, Robin Cross, Ian Lockhart, Terry Kershaw, Philip Robinson, Carl Machin, Richard T Smith, Brian Scott, Christopher Thurstans

Ashfield first year class 1960s (Michael Sargent)

Ashfield rounders c1970 (Michael Sargent)

A lot of pupils transferred after the fourth year to technical college for practical courses which would lead into an apprenticeship. In 1972 the school leaving age got raised to 16. That created some problems because there were people unwillingly staying on. We did try to find practical things for them because they were obviously bored with the classroom.

At Christmas they would invite a number of elderly people in and cook lunch for them and provide entertainment. For two or three years we had quite a large choir which went to Pontefract Music Festival and twice won that and the music teacher built up quite a good band. There were school trips. I tended to take a group to a self catering place, walking, cycling and pony trekking. I was charging £35 and a ski-ing trip was £270.

Michael recalls some of the staff.

The head of science, Bruce Mullin, was seconded to the Nuffield Foundation and invented various bits of apparatus, one of which I think is the Ashfield Ripple Tank. He claimed he invented non drip paint. He mixed two sorts of paint together and they formed a jelly. He wrote to a paint company and a year later this new wonderful non drip paint, came out. But he never patented it.

We'd got one member of staff who was very tall and he used to lift a child up by his elbows and hold him up to his level. He was a gentle giant but children exaggerate and you'd hear horror stories about this member of staff who hung children out of the window because they'd been naughty. But he never did that.

The deputy head had a car accident the year before I went and broke his neck. He had been a tank commander during the war but he referred to every boy as Johnny and every girl as Mary. He had the

Bruce Mullins, head of science, on left, and Clement Tubman take leave of head Ernest Parkinson, with head boy Richard Purcell and head girl Wendy Huffen. 1980s (Michael Sargent)

habit, he would clutch you by the elbow if he was talking to you and wherever he wanted to go, you had to go with him. The biology teacher who came in 1966 had been a lieutenant colonel in the war and by the time he was 25, he'd seen more danger than the majority of people see in a lifetime. Another teacher, his favourite phrase was, "You blockhead". But nothing was meant by it. One other character died only recently, he would have been a professional footballer had it not been for the war. He was still playing football for the staff team at 63, Ben Sowerby. [He died in 2009 at the age of 94. He had played for Sheffield United before the Second World War].

In 1985, some people thought the Sixth Form College should have been on the Archbishop Holgate's site, near to the university, and Ashfield should have remained. But it was going to be the Sixth Form College and we had to disperse. There was a lot of building going on and Acomb Park was being developed. Ashfield would have been the ideal school but they had to go to Millthorpe or Oaklands. We put up a good fight to retain Ashfield as a comprehensive but it was not to be.

Demolition of Ashfield School 1985 (Michael Sargent)

LOWFIELD

Lowfield School opened in Dijon Avenue in 1960 and Ian Johnson attended in his second year, after a year at Acomb Secondary Modern.

I did not want to go to a grammar school. Nobody in the family had gone through the higher education process. We'd all done what was necessary and then got a job. I see nothing wrong in having a system that enables those who are brighter than others to receive an education that's more suited to their level of intelligence. You always get those who fight what is perceived as elitism. If there are ways of enhancing and developing an individual's inherent abilities or

Ian Johnson in dark suit with Mike Burrows, first two boys to sit O levels at Lowfield (Ian Johnson)

intelligence levels, surely that's a good thing. And for those who are lesser able, they're going to need a different approach. There are those who've gone through a secondary education and done very well for themselves, equally those who've gone to grammar school and didn't.

I didn't like Acomb, didn't feel terribly comfortable. It was comparatively old, and huge.

I remember being very inwardly happy at Lowfield. It was smaller in numbers, every teacher knew every pupil. We had a brand new gym, new equipment, nicely varnished. And a sports field. I enjoyed long distance running. We had a photography club. I enjoyed taking photographs from strange angles, altering the light. We'd do our own developing. I used to have a Brownie 127.

I went on to do O levels. In the fourth year there were nine of us but when we got to the fifth, there was only me and this other lad. It wasn't feasible to have a class of two so those pupils who were coming into the fourth year joined us.

By then the school was building up its reputation. The headmaster, John Eyre, said, "I've been talking to one of my neighbours, what do you think about working in a bank?" The upshot was if I got my O levels, there was going to be a job waiting for me. My father

Brownie 127 Camera (Christine Kyriacou)

Name Ian Johnson — Date of Birth **14 - 9 - 49**

REPORT FOR YEAR ENDING ...... *July 1965* ......

AVERAGE AGE OF FORM ......

FORM ...... 5 ...... AGE ... *15 yrs. 11 mths* ......

NUMBER IN FORM .... POSITION IN FORM ......

SUBJECT	Classwork Grade	Exam. Position	REMARKS	TEACHER'S INITIALS
ENGLISH Language			*He is methodical, thorough*	
Literature	B+	B+	*and consistent. Wider reading*	R.W.P.
Composition			*might have improved his*	
			range of ideas but otherwise	
			his progress provides a	
			basis for hopes in GCE:	
MATHEMATICS Arithmetic			*Has worked consistently*	
Algebra	B	B.	*throughout the year*	W.B.
			and attained a	
			promising standard.	
RELIGIOUS INSTR.				
HISTORY	B	B-	*Has worked well though examination*	
			efforts have occasionally been marred	
GEOGRAPHY	B	B	*by insufficient, though however.*	
			Ought to have passed both G.C.E.	
SCIENCE	B	B	*Has worked well and improved his*	C.M.W.
			examination performance to O'level standard	
TECH. DRAWING				
METALWORK				
WOODWORK	B-		*Sound work produced*	W.B.
NEEDLEWORK				
DOMESTIC SCIENCE				

PUNCTUALITY *Excellent*

FORM TEACHER'S REPORT:
Ian is a quiet, well-mannered and reliable boy who works conscientiously at all times.

Signed *E.A. Howell*

HEADMASTER'S REPORT: *Ian has ended a school career of which he can be proud. He should obtain passes in all his ...*

Signed ......

Parent's Signature *L. Johnson*

MODERN SCHOOL

REMARKS	TEACHER'S INITIALS
	R.W.P.

OFFICES, ACHIEVEMENTS, Etc.

Windsor House - Athletics

Ian Johnson's Report (Ian Johnson)

was beside himself. His son working in a bank! He worked at the carriage-works all his life. He was a good bloke, a total gentleman, and all he could think about was his kids doing better than he did.

Ian got six O levels in English, geography, history, general science, maths (arithmetic and algebra), and physics with chemistry (grade 1 CSE).

After a couple of years I joined Yorkshire Insurance. I stayed in insurance and financial services. I do think that the standard of education for maths and English is not as high as it was in my day. You get letters from people : do they know about full stops, commas, and the rest? It is important because it's all about standards.

I'd love to see the old-fashioned apprenticeship ideals being brought back in, an employer responsible for training you to become a plumber or whatever trade, with good old City and Guilds certificates.

In his final report, Ian produced good marks for all subjects with 'excellent' for conduct, appearance, attendance and punctuality. He was a prefect and captain of Windsor House.

If I was leaving school now, I'd seriously consider civil engineering. I'd never heard of the words then. For lasses it was, "Get a shop job, try Terry's or Rowntree's", whatever way you dress it, a menial job. "Do that for a few years, meet a fella, get married, get pregnant". That's your life. You got the odd career person, but that was how it was put over to the majority of girls. You got married and your husband provided. I think the fact that you go through schooling means it's preparing you for life outside. Some schools do it better, but you're mixing with a whole host of other people, and you're highly influenced by that. There's certainly scope for the school to provide some structured approach to life. As a kid you live in the safety environment of the school, from house captain, prefect, top of the tree, you go to your first job and you're immediately at the bottom of the tree. The job I did at the bank, it was called junior.

We're all born equal. We have no prejudices, no favourites, and by the time we go to primary school, there's things you like, things you don't like, people you like or don't like. You get to school, it changes again. Your views about anything, religion, war, food, are fashioned firstly by your parents, secondly your teachers.

Me and my wife were lucky to live through the '60s at the age that we were. We were the first generation of teenagers who were going through this new era of 'everything's great'. Shaking off the final ramifications of the Second World War, money in your pocket, holidays abroad and colour TVs, man on the moon, music, the whole lot. It was a great time to live.

Lowfield School 1970s (Image reproduced courtesy of City of York Council, Local Studies Collection)

Glenn Cockerill attended Carr Primary, then went to Lowfield in 1968, moving to Nunthorpe for the sixth form, so experienced both types of school. He feels that the selection process at 11 was affected by the class system.

Carr had two catchment areas, the middle class area and the more traditional working class area. It seemed to be that if you came from certain areas you were expected to pass the 11 plus, and other areas you were expected to go to a secondary modern. I don't remember any coaching going on. I was led to believe that there was an element of bias in the exam. I was told that certain examples of vocabulary would be recognised in a middle class household but not necessarily in a working class household. We had a choice of secondary moderns and the types available were quite different. I had the choice of Manor, which had a reasonable reputation, Beckfield, which didn't have a very good reputation, or Lowfield which was gaining a good reputation, partly due to the head and some of the staff.

It wasn't a brilliant selection process because quite a few people had failed who maybe shouldn't have. One lad was brilliant at maths and went on to Manchester University and got a really good degree, but because he wasn't very good at English, he failed his 11 plus. One of my best friends at Lowfield, he was fairly middle class, he lived on Stockton Lane, his dad worked his way up to director level. And yet there were people who had passed their 11 plus, and their fathers had a traditional working class occupation. So the lines could be blurred.

At Lowfield they steered you to certain careers that they felt that the majority of people would be capable of. I could see the thinking behind it, that people would be better slotted into certain occupations because you'd think that would work well. But it doesn't necessarily, because they're at such a young age, that you might be putting people in the wrong areas. Some people were earmarked for apprenticeships. The secondary modern schools on this side of the city did have tie-ups at places like the carriage-works.

We had a history teacher that I used to disagree a lot with. We'd have discussions in the fourth and fifth year, we'd do social and economic history from the beginning of the Industrial Revolution. There was a lot of teaching going on but he did allow us to put our point of view especially if there was a current industrial dispute going on which had relevance.

It was felt that I was capable of doing CSEs with O level add-on and I went into the top group. Because the grades that I got were deemed to be good enough, out of the 15 or so in our class, five of us went on to grammar school.

At Lowfield we had a good relationship with the staff. In the fifth year we were given prefect status, there was quite an element of trust. But because you'd had a year of that, going then into the Lower Sixth [at Nunthorpe] where you were just another pupil, was almost a backward step. I couldn't believe some of the things I was hearing, with discipline, just high jinks and stupidity. Lowfield had very strong discipline. I'm not saying things didn't happen but it was certainly nipped in the bud. I found a lot of immaturity at Nunthorpe. They just couldn't cope with seeing girls in close proximity. We'd been used to it, and had quite a few girls as friends. But they were probably more mature [at Nunthorpe] in other ways. We'd talk about things like politics whereas there'd only been a small group of us at Lowfield that would be interested in it.

The sporting side was very good, they used to excel in county competitions. Probably sports is the one area where secondary modern schools could compete on an equal footing. I did actually represent Nunthorpe at athletics, the sprint. And I did a lot of triple jumps. At Nunthorpe I learnt a lot, I made some good friends, it did change me in many ways but it was disappointing from an academic point of view. You didn't get the help that you'd got. You were in bigger classes. You were expected to do the learning on your own. And it wasn't an environment that I was used to. But it widened my horizons. I started mixing with people who had a broader outlook on life. I started going to the theatre and going to see Shakespeare. We had an inter school sixth form society, and they'd get together with other schools and have dances. We had the Edgar Broughton Band the year before I left.

The problem with some schools, they were assuming that because you hadn't passed the 11 plus, the majority of people didn't have any gifts or talents. Yet a lot of them did, but they weren't allowed to express them or they weren't being brought out, and that is such a waste. Almost everyone is gifted or talented in one area. I thought Sixth Form College was a really good idea because it meant that everybody was starting from a level playing field. I was in favour of comprehensive schools, that people would be mixing together.

Glenn became a quantity surveyor.

You could get A levels and do a degree, but I did day release, ONC and then HNC. At Lowfield, I probably wouldn't have even thought about doing that. It was contacts I'd made at Nunthorpe that enabled me to get a job as a junior quantity surveyor.

Lowfield became comprehensive in 1985. Oaklands School came to merge with Lowfield in 2003 to form York High School, whilst the new

school was being built at Cornlands Road to accommodate 1000 pupils. The building at Dijon Avenue finally closed its doors in summer 2007, with a farewell assembly and release of balloons. Lowfield School was left empty, but fire attacks in 2008 and 2009 led to its demolition in 2010.

The site of Lowfield School after demolition 2010 (Oliver Bostock)

DERWENT

Derwent opened in 1959 with 172 pupils, and until 1972 was governed jointly with Danesmead Secondary Modern. By 1962 there were 370 pupils. In 1965, the BBC made a film of the school entitled 'Portrait of a Secondary Modern School'. By 1967 the Teacher's World described the teachers as having 'the ability to direct youthful enthusiasms and sympathies into creative channels'. From the beginning, the pupils were encouraged to have a social conscience, raising funds for various charities, providing Christmas meals for pensioners, and one form adopted a low income family and provided a turkey and Christmas gifts. Community service was part of the curriculum with senior pupils visiting the elderly and infirm in the area. In the 1970s a ukulele club was formed, and a young ornithologist's club. Pupils went skiing, sailed down the Rhine and took part in the Lyke Wake Walk. Most schools relied on the Parent Teacher Association to raise funds for extra curricular activities. In the 1970s, they raised money for a minibus garage, canoes, stage lights, curtains, props and costumes. The school magazines describe walks across the North Yorkshire Moors with an army team, climbing Helvellyn, a moving visit to the new Coventry Cathedral, and trips to London and Paris.

Eileen Carter was born in 1938 and attended St George's Junior School and then Bar Convent Grammar.

Derwent School Staff 1970s. Eileen Carter third left on front row (Eileen Carter)

It was a big thing, the 11 plus, because if you didn't pass you were a failure. Grammar schools certainly open doors that you wouldn't get from a secondary modern, when you left at 15. If you wanted to carry on, you went to Technical College. My mother was a great reader and encouraged us, and was a firm believer in education. When I went for the interview at Queen Anne's for the borderline children, you had no idea what you were going to get asked. They brought a picture out and you had to look at it and answer questions. And they asked what you wanted to be. From out of the blue I said, "A teacher". I think that swayed it. The girl with me said shorthand and typing and she didn't get in.

Eileen worked in several offices and later went to train as a mature student at James Graham College in Leeds before teaching at Derwent.

Money wise it was very tight at college. I lived at home and travelled daily. It was thanks to the support of Mum and Dad that I could do that but I did casual jobs to earn money. It was much more vigorous than it is now. You had to do a main subject for three years to virtually degree level, you had to do English for two years, a basic course in maths and science, two subsidiary subjects, I did art and PE. Then the history of education, philosophy, psychology, sociology and also teaching practice. When I came out and got a job I was earning less as a teacher than I'd been earning as a civil servant. I did teaching practice at Derwent. You couldn't apply to individual schools, you applied to York City Education Committee. They would offer you a job but wouldn't guarantee which school. I actually got Derwent. I started off teaching history and English.

When I came into teaching, you could see there were a lot of children at the top end of secondary moderns that were just as good as kids at the bottom end of grammar schools. You could have interchanged them without any problem. We got a lot of children who did very well at O levels and went on to sixth form in grammar school. We worked hard and I taught 38 out of 40 periods in my probationary year. I had two free periods of 35 minutes for preparation. I took 40 kids on a bus to the Castle Museum in my first week.

It seems that grammar schools had more resources and more facilities.

Fifth years youth hostelling in 1970s, Eileen Carter third from left (Eileen Carter)

And more money. Why? We taught the bulk of the kids, and got the least resources. The money should have been evenly spread and we should have all had a fair crack of the whip. Derwent was a smallish school. We did get up to 500 when they raised the leaving age. There was a real family atmosphere. We had some really good kids. I went with the English man and took them youth hostelling.

A lot of secondary moderns did well because they were smaller, there

Fifth years by a river, youth hostelling in 1970s, Eileen Carter second from right in centre.
(Eileen Carter)

was a lot of dedicated teachers and the kids responded. You were going to have some difficult kids and kids who weren't going to do anything. But there was a lot of opportunity for kids who wanted to do something. They got a lot more attention. A lot of grammar school kids that didn't achieve, would have done so in our environment. In secondary moderns [there was] *an understanding of their backgrounds and what they could and couldn't afford.*

I taught a lot of kids who weren't academic and some of them struggled but we did all sorts of things with them. I was head of Integrated Studies. We took them to Hull Docks, Bradford Industrial Museum, the Treasurer's House, on river trips. We did traffic surveys, job interviews, a lot of music and shows and plays. You can't do that now, everything's prescriptive about the National Curriculum. We used to do day release. They decided what they would like to do, and did it maybe for two years before they finished.

Rounders team at Derwent 1969. Eileen Carter centre of back row (Eileen Carter)

Hockey team at Derwent, includes Carolyn Airey, Sally Allison, Linda Clarke, Liz Cook, Nancy Dodds, Judith Harrison, Susan Howarth, Janet King, Elizabeth Oldfield, Jane Potter, Lynda Richmond, Susan Webster, Judith Wrightson 1970s (Eileen Carter)

Girls did netball, rounders and hockey. Boys did rugby and football. And we did softball, tennis and badminton, and athletics. We had a track. It's now got housing on it. I remember one girl coming up to me, "I've bought a house miss, it's right on the goal where we played hockey". It was after school and Saturday for sports rallies. That was done by staff who weren't just PE, they would take a team, train them, do athletics or rounders. Then it all stopped when Mr Baker brought in his 1,265 hours for teachers to teach. The staff lost five days holiday and so a lot of them stopped the voluntary activity. Now I wouldn't take kids out. The pages you have to fill in, health and safety risks. Common sense has gone out of the window and we've got the suing culture now.

GAMES CAPTAIN

I know one or two from Derwent who went on to be teachers. One boy went to Archbishop's to do A levels and became head boy and went on to university. They got a lot of help and encouragement and their families were very keen because they were upset if a child didn't get the 11 plus. I think a lot of their natural abilities came out and they got the opportunity and used it. Mr Tudor, the head, was quite a legend. He started the school and was head of Park Grove before he came. He was very forward thinking, determined to do the best for his pupils, regardless of academic ability. We had fun and you could have a bit of relaxation with the kids, although we were pretty strict.

When they decided to become comprehensive, they closed Derwent. We amalgamated with Archbishop's and there were still some of the grammar school boys left. There was about 900 with the amalgamation and it was very difficult because staff came from different schools. A lot of our children were very resentful. But it was a fait accompli and that was it. It was a real hotch potch towards the end.

Neal Guppy taught at Derwent.

Neal Guppy at Guppy's Club 1960s
(Neal Guppy)

I loved the fact first of all of boys and girls together. It takes men all their time to understand women, through the whole length of life. Having cut away from them at 11 to 17 seemed silly to me and it didn't help at all. So the atmosphere within the secondary modern school was a very happy one. I think the girls softened things. I was very fortunate it had a strong leadership by Doug Tudor.

It was streamed in certain subjects. They went through an experiment in the early '70s when the education authorities decided that streaming should be out. They went onto project work where you had six teachers sharing the work and it was a disaster because if you get a teacher off ill then they can't carry the responsibility of their area. The theory was that the fast learning student would help the slow learning student. But they'd not allowed for human nature, and the fast learner became irritated with having to slow down and help somebody all the time, rather than learn at the speed of their own capacity.

I loved it at Derwent. I would have carried on if I hadn't had the opportunity to run my club, [Guppy's club for young people]. *In my last year, we started to take O levels. I taught physics, chemistry and biology. The emphasis was more on physics. Lads enjoy mechanical things, electrical things, gadgets. Girls are more concerned with the biology and the animal side of things, by and large. I was teaching how fuses work in the system, for practical purposes and this girl was taking no interest whatsoever. I said, "You want to learn this. You're at home, you want to iron your dress before you go out on a Friday night, your parents are out and a fuse goes. What are you going to do?" "Oh that's easy sir, I'll go to the next door neighbour and ask him to do it!" There's a very deep lesson there about the relationship between males and females. In many ways she's right, that's what happens.*

I always think within education that if you can show people something that applies practically to their lives, you may be able then to move on to more academic stuff. That's often missing, particularly in maths and algebra, it's taught and you think, "What the hell am I going to use that for?" You learn what you think might be useful. If you are naturally academic, maybe you will take an interest in something quite obscure, but most of us don't unless we see why it is relative.

I used to take them out for botany and biology classes. All you had to do was go to the head and say, "It's a lovely day, I'm thinking of going out to Tang Hall beck and see what we can find". "Off you go,

Neal, that's fine". You can't do that today. You've got to apply weeks or months before to get your insurance covered by the authority. And then of course it's pouring down on the day you want to go.

Being brought through the academic system, you got used to the set-up there, and when I got a lad swearing in the class, it didn't ruffle my feathers. Often teachers, because a lad had sworn, got very upset and sent the boy to the headmaster. I didn't, because I recognised that that was colloquial language in the household. So although I didn't accept it as routine, if it happened occasionally, I was more likely to say, "That's enough", and not get upset. The sports teacher who was at college with me, the system he had, "Behave yourself or you miss your sports", and that's a much more positive way of dealing with it. Occasionally in my class I held them in and very occasionally I caned, if somebody did something really way out and dangerous.

Some of the youngsters who weren't academic had a kind of animal wisdom about life, and so it's a two way process all the time. I had such good fun when I was teaching and it was a lovely school, everybody belonged and he was a damn good headmaster, Mr Tudor.

It's important to have children learn to the best of their ability, so it does mean that there are certain subjects where streaming should take place. I do believe in a comprehensive system, the 11 plus had the stigma that 20 per cent were successful and 80 per cent were failures, that's illogical. I gained a lot of experience in the army through mixing with people of different academic abilities. I hadn't had the chance of meeting them as I would have done in a comprehensive school. I didn't believe in the 11 plus as such but I do believe in testing so you know where you are on the scale of things.

The school magazine in 1983 reported on the varied careers of its ex-pupils. Two old boys were on ships that went down during the Falklands war, both survived, and others had become soldiers, sailors and airmen, worked in Canada, in Israel on a kibbutz, or were teaching in USA and Germany. There were models, press photographer, stage manager, dancer

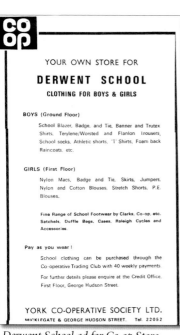

Derwent School ad for Co-op Store
(Eileen Carter)

with the Northern Ballet Company, professional musicians, nursing sisters, chefs, mechanics, engineers, policemen, artists, civil servants, a professional rugby player, research astronomer, lab technician, mechanics, and a hotel reception supervisor in a big London hotel.

Derwent seems to have had a caring and almost family atmosphere. Teacher Monica Black recalled, in the school magazine, that her happiest memory was of,

hearing the voices of Derwent girls singing 'O Come Down Love Divine' as I walked down the aisle of St Olave's church for my wedding. That was something very precious.

MANOR SCHOOL

A school to promote the education of the poor was founded in 1812 in the Merchant Taylor's Hall, which split the following year into a girls' school at Aldwark and boys' school at King's Manor. Pupils had to pay one shilling a quarter. Attendance was required on Sundays and even the morning of Christmas Day, and in 1819 it was resolved that 'a plum cake costing 2d be given to each child, and that absentees be punished'. The Yorkshire School for the Blind also occupied part of the building from 1833. Discipline was strict at the Manor School and the record for November 1882 shows that 'three boys were caned for truanting, four for climbing, four for damaging the Blind School property and six for not arriving until noon'. In 1915 the building was requisitioned by the Army Pay Department, and the school moved to Haxby Road School. By the end of the First World War, 36 old boys had died. In 1922 the school purchased the former York Industrial School in Marygate for £3,800 and in 1926 was given the status of a higher grade school. By 1932 there were 400 boys.

Unfortunately in 1942, the school was hit in the Baedeker air raid on York and moved to Priory Street, merging with the girls' school there in 1947 to become a mixed school. The Model School closed in 1964 and the 64 pupils transferred to Manor, which moved to its new site at Low Poppleton Lane the following year. In 1985 it was enlarged to take on its role as a comprehensive school.

Douglas Church was born in 1920 and was at the school from 1930 to 1934. He remembers the discipline.

Douglas Church 1950s
(Douglas Church)

You used to have to go to the headmaster's study if you misbehaved and he'd cane you, but often they'd cane you in class if you did something wrong.

There was a swimming bath down below the school and that's where I learnt to swim. It was very cold down in the basement. You'd to sit on the side of the baths and Mrs Gibson would push you in. She was in charge of swimming and also PT. I must admit some of the men teachers were chasing her and thought her attractive, very well made.

In the morning the large room was where you used to call the assembly, all the classes would come in and say their prayers. It was also the gymnasium. It had a cabinet full of curios which old scholars had brought back from different foreign countries, like snakes in preservatives, in this glass case.

There was one long corridor in alignment from end to end, the left hand side was the sunny side. The opposite side was quite dark. Fortunately I spent most of my time in the sunny side. I was up early in the morning to take the papers out, and I'd get a bit tired and when the sun was shining through, often I used to fall off to sleep. And I'd get caned. We had four different houses - Manor, Abbey, Wentworth and Stuart. [Today there are six, the two new ones are Priory and King's]. *And we'd have a board on the classroom wall and each class used to contest to see who could get the most marks. I did history, maths, art, French, chemistry, English and geography. I wasn't bad at maths, but I wasn't very good at French. We had a very bad tempered master. He'd call you all kinds of names if you didn't get your verbs correct. I didn't get along very well with him, I must admit, he called me 'idiot' and 'imbecile'. I came quite high in shorthand and book-keeping and I passed two Pitman's exams, one for theory and one for 40 words per minute.*

We used to go to the chemistry place, the laboratory. The teacher Stinky Bell looked as though he was dying on his feet. He looked like Gandhi, the chap that used to wear loincloths. He had Bunsen burners and different equipment and made smells but he never showed any enthusiasm. Some teachers do inspire you, some teachers do strike a chord. If you're on the same wavelength you can react to them. History was one of my favourite subjects. I used to read a lot at home. It put me in good standing, and when we got asked a question, I knew the answer. He was all right, was Rutherford, [the teacher] *he bought me a book when I left, for good work in history.*

Manor Badge (Katie Bonney)

Most of the boys got on quite well. They did fall into groups, kind of gangs. On the whole they didn't persecute you, except silly things like pulling your hat off and throwing it on the roof. You used to have a cap with the coat of arms on. You weren't forced to wear uniform. There was a jacket but most of the parents hadn't the money to buy it. We'd have a slide there, used to slide down the playground in winter time with the frost. We'd play for hours with conkers but they can't do that now. They penalise everybody because of one or two that get hurt. We used to have a school concert, every back end, and they were really good. They'd do plays and satires.

I was 14 when I left. There was no careers teacher to advise you on what kind of job you should take. I went to my uncle's and I was a butcher's boy for a short while before I went to an apprenticeship as a plumber. That was all the thing then, apprenticeships. If you could get in one, you were lucky. Six years after I left school, I was called up in 1940, and went in the army.

The Manor's reputation for sporting excellence in the 1930s led to it winning the All School's cup for football for five successive years.

Ken Humphreys was born in 1933 and attended a boys' grammar school, then did teacher training at St John's College.

In 1957 I was appointed to Manor Church of England School in Priory Street as the geography teacher. And I took the boys for rugby, which involved walking to the Knavesmire, hanging your coats over the wire fence, hoping it was fine, and doing your best to dodge what the cows had left behind. We had a well established wet-weather programme which the children didn't like because it consisted of either maths or RE. Monday always started with a service at Holy Trinity Church. Dinners were taken in Wesley Chapel next door. Then we had speech night in the Tempest Anderson Hall.

Manor was an old fashioned school where everybody was on top of everybody else. It was small. Most of today's schools are far too large. Manor hasn't grown out of all proportion but you get a school with 11 or 1200 children, 100 on the staff, there'll be some of the staff don't know all the staff, never mind the children.

It had a good reputation. The biggest problem was the building [in Priory Street]. *It couldn't compare to the schools like Burnholme, Beckfield Lane, all fairly modern buildings with loads of playing field space. We had two buildings, the new building and the old. They should have been called the old and the ancient. It was '65 when we actually made the move, it was November, and it was pouring down. We just moved lock, stock and barrel. The facilities were very different. The church spent an enormous amount of money. A beautiful gym and the roof was pitched and consisted of strips of wood which would all have to be individually nailed. It was a work of art.*

Once we moved, the connection we'd had with St Olave's, Marygate, ceased. The Bishop of Selby became automatically chairman of governors. And then when we needed a church service, we walked to the Holy Redeemer on Boroughbridge Road. Although in the hall, the lads in the metalwork shop had made a nice altar table with cross and candlestick on a raised dais.

We took the children to Oberammergau for the passion play in 1970. That was quite an affair, that was lovely. A week in Saltzburg first, then to see the play.

The wood carver, Dick Reid, taught at Manor at this time.

He was a snorting fella, so talented. He once dragged me really out of the mire. The headmaster came in and said, "You've got one of the senior classes. A marquee has arrived, will you and the boys go and put it up?" I thought, "What the hell do I know about erecting a marquee?" But I knew Dick was in the Territorial Army and he was just next door so I bobbed round and, "All right Ken, you watch this lot and I'll take care of it". I hadn't a clue, I'd have been there yet.

We were one of the first schools to get a television, in the day when it wasn't all that common. We took it up to the new school. It was a great big thing, looked like a wardrobe, great big doors. One of the workmen said, "Have you any idea where this is going to go?"

"Yes it's going in my room". But then, "There isn't a television point in the school". So they'd built a brand new school and hadn't put a television point in. So they had to put an aerial up and bring it down the outside wall and in through the window frame into room six.

They decided to put the fire alarm box on the wall inside the gym. You can guess what happened. As soon as the lads saw it, they decided they'd go down the far end of the room with a football and see if they could hit it. Then they put the clock in the gym immediately above the basketball ring. One day one of the lads just overshot a bit, it clipped the top of the board, hit the clock and came down on the gym floor with a noise like you've never heard. Then they put a new clock up there and covered it with wire mesh which was so closely knit, you couldn't tell what time it was.

At the new school, the meals were cooked on the spot, not brought in, in containers, that was another big difference. The senior girls, when they were doing cookery, could invite a member of staff to lunch. I was lucky because I got on very well with the children. I got asked more than anybody else. They'd open the door and escort you to the table and give you a two course lunch and make sure everything was just so.

Ken got on well with his pupils and was always a listening ear for anyone with a problem. He recalls a delicate time with one of the girls he taught.

Two girls came to see me. One of them said, "Can we have a word sir? It's A, she's expecting". We had a chat about that. "I can't tell my mother, she'll kill me". She said she was going away for the weekend to stay with a friend and while she was away she got rid of it. Then when she came back to school, she came to me and said, "It's PE, sir, and I can't do it". I said to the lady PE teacher, "I'm not going into any detail but A won't be doing PE today, she's not very well".

I did 28 years at Manor, then in 1985 when we went comprehensive, they took the opportunity to move nearly everybody. Anybody who was 55 or over was offered early retirement with five years enhancement on salary. I was 51. We had to go to a series of interviews as to where they would appoint you. I finished up at Oaklands. But there weren't more than three or four of the staff actually remained at Manor.

The people who found it particularly difficult were the people who had taught in the grammar schools because of the type of child you were going to come across. As regards myself, the only difference it made was that I was going to be teaching some child who was a little bit brighter. But you had some teachers who'd concentrated on sixth form, who might have been teaching very small groups of children who were clever and wanted to learn. Suddenly they were faced with 26 sixteen year olds, some of whom wished they were anywhere but at school. It was quite common for them to last one or two terms.

Being a church school, it did make a difference when we went comprehensive, because we were only 500 yards from Beckfield Lane Secondary. Beckfield had much better facilities, an enormous area, playing fields, buildings in good order. They had a music block. But there was no question about which one was going to close. You could close a state school when somebody signed a bit of paper. But to close a church school would have practically required an act of parliament. And within months you would never have known that there'd been a school there because it was covered in houses.

Katie Appleby 1962 (Katie Bonney)

Katie Bonney (née Appleby)

was born in 1948 and went to St Clement's Junior School. My mother said, "I hope you don't pass your 11 plus because we'd have to buy you a uniform". But I wanted to go to Manor. It was in Priory Street then. I was a bit of a tomboy so a girls' school was not for me. I was in the A stream all the way through. Mr

Gym team at Manor. Back row L to R – Pamela Robinson, Katie Appleby, Agnes Scutt, Ann Turnbull, Susan Barber, Shirley Stilgoe. Front row – Carol Miller, Judith Walker, Pat Ibbotson, Susan Broadhead, Margaret Pinder (Katie Bonney)

Humphreys was my geography teacher and I thoroughly enjoyed geography as it was taught in those days. The countries, the capitals, the infrastructure, it was so interesting.

My only trip with the school was to Switzerland in 1961. It was a lovely experience. We did a lot of walking, up the lanes and the meadows with the cows, very different to all the flat land of York. My father worked on the railway so I got to the border of Switzerland for free. You had to pay for the accommodation and the transport there.

We did music with Mr Gladders, 'lips, teeth and tips of tongues' was his saying. [He taught at the school for 36 years]. *Housecraft was very different. I made a little needle case, a compact case. We had to learn to turn a sheet so if there was a split, how you would repair it. We made a very simple dress. We didn't just do cooking, you had to learn how to clean a hairbrush properly, how to clean a cooker not just use it. We made aprons, had to wash them and learn to starch, before spray cans.*

We didn't do homework, Mr Fieldsend didn't approve. We never learnt another language. I was head girl for my sins, because I was the oldest prefect. I was in charge of the girls' corridor. We walked on the left upstairs. It was only for discipline, and ringing the bell when it was the end of playtime. You seemed to recognise the faces. "Watch

Badge for York School of Commerce
(Katie Bonney)

that one, she goes up two steps at a time". That wasn't allowed. The head boy was watching the boys' stairs. Never the twain should meet. And the girls sat at one side of the room, the boys sat at the other.

We had discussions within the class. And everybody listened to what anybody had to say, there was no gossip while somebody else was talking. Unless you were in the science room, that was very different. It was fun as well as being informative.

Boys from Manor School examining replica Viking tools during Coppergate excavation 1978, with site director Richard Hall holding 13th century original, probably a manure fork (Newsquest North East Ltd)

I went to Commercial College in Nessgate for two years, where Fenwick's is before that was newly vamped. It was after 16 so it was further education. I did shorthand and typing and English. There were maybe four of us, and a couple of lads went [from Manor]. It was very big compared to Manor. My sister went to Commerce College and ended up at the Northern Command offices. She got an extremely good job and she always said that Manor set her in good stead. The teachers couldn't do enough for you, they encouraged you. You could always approach them, they wanted you to progress.

Manor's final move was in 2009 to Millfield Lane, and the numbers grew from 640 to 920 pupils. The head teacher Brian Crosby described the new school (which cost £18 million) as 'modern, colourful, vibrant, light and spacious…more like a college campus'. The school is now a specialist Performing Arts College and has recently applied to be an 'academy'.

CHAPTER 7

INDEPENDENT SCHOOLS

Although York had many small private schools in the years up to the Second World War, after the war there were only four independent secondary schools, Bootham and St Peter's for boys, and The Mount and York College for Girls. All of them took scholarship pupils as well as those who were fee-paying.

St Peter's School in Clifton claims to be the oldest school in England. In the 1930s it consisted of three departments – classical, modern and junior, with special arrangements for those who wished to take up medicine, law or qualify for Sandhurst (the Army), Woolwich (the naval college) or Cranwell (the RAF). After 1919, St Peter's admitted five scholarship boys each year. After centuries of being an all boys' school, girls were admitted to the sixth form in 1976, and then right through the school in 1987. In 1900 there were 65 boys in the school, in 1999 there were 491 girls and boys.

The Mount School was founded as a boarding school in Trinity Lane in 1785, then housed in Castlegate. In 1857 it moved to its present site in Dalton Terrace. It is unique in the United Kingdom, combining a co-educational junior department with a girls' senior school with a Quaker ethos. The Mount is the last single sex secondary school in York.

The Mount and St Peter's have been well covered in other publications so this study will use Bootham and York College for Girls as examples of York's independent schools.

YORK COLLEGE FOR GIRLS

In 1880, a school was opened by the Girls' Public Day School Company in Fishergate House, which moved in 1900 to 69 Low Petergate, a

York College for Girls
(Church Schools)   and Kindergarten
  Co., Ltd.

Patron :
His Grace The Archbishop of York.
The College is under the shadow of
the Minster and has a Hostel for
Boarders in one of the best residential
suburbs of the City. Sound education
on Public School lines. Girls prepared for the Universities and all
Qualifying Examinations.
Definite Church teaching.
Three Scholarships offered annually,
one restricted to daughters of Clergy-
men.

E. E. ELLETT
(Oxf. Hon. Mods. Maths.), Head Mistress.

Advertisement from York Guide
(Mike Race)

residence originally built in 1725 for John Shaw, Proctor of the Court at York. The school closed in 1907. The York Church High School for Girls, founded in 1891 in Minster Yard, was owned by the Church Schools' Company and in January 1908 it moved into 69 Low Petergate to become York College for Girls, an independent day school. From 1919 there was accommodation for 30 boarders at Burton Grange in Clifton but this had closed by the 1930s. In an advertisement in the 1930 Guide to York, the school promised that 'pupils receive a sound general education suitable as a preparation for any career they may choose'.

A number of eminent ladies were educated at the school, including politicians, lawyers and doctors, the most famous being Dame Janet Baker, the highly acclaimed opera and concert singer, who was there

York College for Girls pre 1908 at Minster Yard (La Vecchia Scuola)

during the Second World War and made her stage debut in 1956. She was Chancellor of York University from 1991 to 2004, having become a Dame Commander of the British Empire in 1976 and a Companion of Honour in 1993.

Margaret Mann Phillips, the first pupil to go to Oxford and daughter of the Rector of St Margaret's Church, Walmgate, (now the Early Music Centre), wrote a history of the school covering the years 1919-1924, when it flourished under the formidable headmistress, Elizabeth Emma Ellett, known to the girls as 'E cubed'. She expected the highest academic standards and Margaret Mann did not disappoint. She gained a first in French at Oxford, and later a doctorate in Paris, going on to become a lecturer at Newnham College, Cambridge and a leading authority on Erasmus and Renaissance literature.

Two different inns have existed on the site of York College for Girls. The school's Talbot Room with its beautiful fireplace was once part of the seventeenth century Talbot Inn, taken down in 1730. The Fox Inn closed in 1955 and in 1960 a new building was opened where the Fox had

York College girls with Miss E. E. Ellett (E cubed) (La Vecchia Scuola)

School in Low Petergate in 1930s (Newsquest North East Ltd)

been, to house the chapel, library, science labs, home economics room and classrooms. In 1981 the school expanded further down Petergate towards King's Square, to house the music wing, more classrooms and laboratories.

After a prolonged battle by staff, pupils and parents, the school closed its doors in 1997, with 234 pupils moving elsewhere. Services at the beginning and end of term were held in the Minster so it was fitting that the last service at the school took place in the Lady Chapel there.

When the school closed, York Civic Trust and the Old Girls' Association were concerned that the three panels of stained glass in the chapel, by one of the most important stained glass artists of the 20th century, Harry Stammers, (who had a studio in Gray's Court) should be preserved. They had been installed when the school was refurbished in the 1950s.

Fortunately, the owners of the building allowed the panels to be removed and installed in the undercroft of the Merchant Adventurer's Hall. The triptych features the Annunciation, and Stammers used the Dean of York as a model for one of the shepherds.

Excavation of Talbot Rooms 2004. Early 17th century fireplace (York Archaeological Trust)

York Archaeological Trust undertook an excavation on the site of the school in 2004-5, uncovering post-medieval buildings and a complex sequence of medieval workshops dating from the 13th to 15th centuries. The archaeologist in charge, Field Officer Ben Reeves,

first went to the site as a digger when Mark Johnson was in charge. I spent some time exploring the rooms. It was a labyrinth of a building, and quite disorientating, being several structures dating from the 15th century to the 1950s, all connected over the years, through passages and doorways, all on slightly different levels. I supervised the demolition of the prefab buildings [where the gymnasium

Stained glass window from the school chapel
(Company of Merchant Adventurers of City of York, Photographer : Jeremy Phillips)

was housed] *to the rear of the main building and then directed the excavation on the piece of ground where they had stood. We uncovered building remains in four medieval tenements and evidence for leather, copper-alloy metal and bone working. We had also been commissioned to record the buildings, as new internal fabric was uncovered daily during the alterations. During the recording a small bottle of Gordon's gin, probably dating from the 1960s, was found secreted amongst the rafters in the attic. Maybe this was contraband smuggled in by a rebellious pupil, or perhaps it shows that teaching has always been a stressful job and this was a secret staff tipple hidden away for the end of a difficult day!*

Today the building is an Italian restaurant named La Vecchia Scuola, 'The Old School', with apartments on the floors above.

Excavation 2004 *(York Archaeological Trust)*

Anne Ellison attended the school in 1944. She recalls the grand entrance with pillars on the front of Petergate.

You went in there on the first day, taken by your parents. After that we went in by the back entrance. It was totally a rabbit warren. The present conservatory is built into the playground. You can see the original walls. Schools in those days were very much boys' schools or girls' schools. In the hall was a shelf for each house, and house cups were displayed there. There was a competitive spirit. We had prizes for different subjects at speech day. For morning prayers,

Excavation of rear of school 2005
(York Archaeological Trust)

*the headmistress was on the platform. We were in our form blocks,
the staff at the end of the rows, and we sat on the floor crosslegged.
When we had drama events, they would put curtains up. At the back
of the platform, there were honours boards for people who had gone
to university.*

*We were very involved in the Minster, it was our school church. For
Ascension Day we went there, came back for breakfast and had the
rest of the day off.*

In 1952, Anne went to Newcastle University, at a time when only a
minority of women, certainly in York, went on to university.

*I had to work very hard. I was keen to go and I enjoyed it a lot.
It was a very small sixth form, only about six or eight at the most.
Geography and biology were my subjects and there were only two of
us doing geography.*

*We still had rationing, (and at university you got a supply of butter
and sugar put in your room on a Monday and that had to last you
for the week). The war had been over six years but we were still
living a very austere life. Our mothers gave up an awful lot for us,
they'd go without certain foods so the children were getting a bit
more. For uniform we had to go to Southcott's. There were quite a lot
of hand me downs. We had lisle stockings in the winter which became
quite wrinkly.*

*When you go into the restaurant now, Miss [Helena] Randall's office
was on the right which is now the bar. Each term, you went in one
by one to be handed your report. You weren't allowed to open it. It
was sealed and your parents' name on it. The headmistress seemed
very old to me, but in fact she was born in 1900, so she was 44.
She looked as if she was in her 60s, her hair was always grey and
she did it in a bun. I remember Mrs Elliot was very inspirational
with geography, Miss Corr was our English teacher, a very vivacious
person. As it was a small school, you had your own group of friends*

but you knew other people as well, and you would go to their birthday parties. If it [the school] comes up in conversation, people will say, "You were the lucky one".

Anne was at school with Dame Janet Baker.

If you stood next to Janet, you knew she had a different voice to everybody else. The singing teacher at the time, Miss Barber, said she had 'gold in her throat'. And how right she was. Janet worked for Barclays Bank and then went into singing professionally.

When York College was going to close, there had been discussions about the College and the Mount going to amalgamate. They hadn't discussed this with the parents, and the parents didn't want this. They wanted to choose where to send their children. I felt if York College was going to close, it should close as the school with the reputation it had, rather than just move off to the Mount.

I think if Erica Taylor [the last head teacher] had been there sooner, it might not have closed. Erica had great presence as a head teacher, she had a much stronger voice. But I think the spadework had all been done. The parents fought very hard for the school not to close. But the Church Schools' had made up their mind. A lot of us wrote to them, I never had a reply and I felt that was very bad. It was a happy school, we had fun. I think it was very sad it closed.

Dame Janet Baker (Dame Janet Baker)

The Old Girls' Association has over 200 members.

We have a committee in York and arrange events like going to Hovingham Hall, Harlow Carr, Burnby Gardens. A lot of members are spread around the country. I still have friends from school in London, America, one in Tasmania. Of my form, there are just three of us living in York.

Mary Collier (née Tugwell) was born in 1937, and started in 1943 in the junior school.

During the war, we had a large air raid shelter which was earth covered. We used to go down as a practice. It was open at both ends. But you weren't allowed to climb on top of the grass. It seemed to take up an awful lot of the playground. I remember going into York the day after the Blitz in 1942 and seeing buildings blackened and firemen around. We had windows cracked or blasted out.

The school day started with prayers which usually the headmistress took on the stage. There was a baby grand piano, and quite often one of the pupils would play it. There was a lectern and a very nice Mousey Thompson table and chair. [From Robert Thompson at Kilburn, whose trade mark was a small mouse].

I was only interested in sport. At the end of the school year, it was read out whether you had got your school colours, and for which sport. One of the most coveted colours was for deportment. It was an ongoing thing. Your appearance, tidiness, general demeanour and the way you spoke to people. You could have elocution lessons one to one.

The shields were green, then you had blue colours for St Andrew's house, yellow for St David's and red for St George's. I did netball, cricket, hockey, swimming, rounders. Netball was in the playground. The hall was used for a badminton court. For tennis we walked to Bootham School. We also had a ground in Burton Stone Lane for hockey. We had our sports day there.

Boater from 1960 *(La Vecchia Scuola)*   Scarf, tie and badges from school *(La Vecchia Scuola)*

But this was a ladies' school, I don't think sport was held in great [esteem]. I got the 'Service to the School' prize when I left, because I had been secretary for sports and would contact other schools when we played inter school matches. And the prize was shared for the first time, because it usually went to the head girl.

When it came to doing plays, they had to improvise with the girls. I remember doing 'A Midsummer Night's Dream' and we used the Dean's garden. I wasn't in it, I would get involved with costumes or lighting.

The mistress I liked best was the sports mistress, Miss Morrell. She got polio. We were at Rowntree's pool, practising for the swimming gala, and the next morning she didn't come in to school. She was in the isolation hospital in an iron lung and that's where she stayed for three years and she died. We raised money to buy her a page turning machine. She couldn't do anything but move her little finger and this machine would turn the page of a book. I stopped competitive swimming because of the polio in York. They thought it was pool water that was the carrier.

We lived a privileged life but there was still rationing. There was a shop in the school and you could get second hand blazers. We had gym tunics with green velvet round the top and big box pleats, and big green knickers with elastic round the bottom and long legs, and liberty bodices, white socks and Clark's brown sandals in summer.

We were taken to the Gas showrooms for cookery, [in Blake Street]. We used to sit in rows and watch them cook, we didn't actually get our hands dirty.

They were quite strict there, if you were seen out without your beret on, we did get detentions. I remember one of our form becoming pregnant. It was never really mentioned. She just disappeared. That was in the early 50s. I left in '54 and went nursing in 1955. The headmistress's real hope was that you would go to university. When my third sister went to see her and she said she was going nursing as the other two had, she said, "Can't the Tugwell family do anything but nurse?"

When the school closed,

we were very upset. It was out of the blue but I think the rot set in when Bootham and St Peter's started taking girls. While they were boys' schools, York College flourished. I'm sure York is the poorer for not having it.

Gillian Sowray went to Fishergate Primary School and in 1968,

although I was in the top three, I managed to fail my 11 plus. I did the entrance exam for York College for Girls, it had a good reputation, and music was my main interest. It was harder than the 11 plus so I was quite surprised to pass it and be offered a place. I was used to 30 plus in a class at Fishergate and suddenly I was in a small school, less than 200 pupils.

Gillian Sowray c1973 (Gillian Sowray)

The entrance on Petergate was only for visitors. Sixth form and staff used the entrance to the side but the others used the back entrance. The staircases were all higgledy piggledy, there were panels, interesting brickwork and fireplaces. The Talbot Room was used as a rehearsal room. I remember going out of the window there once which you weren't supposed to do. It was at ground level, I just took it as a short cut. I stayed for school dinners. I didn't mind them. We had the usual sort of stew, sausages or shepherd's pie. Butterscotch tart was always a favourite, and rice pudding and rosehip syrup.

We had rules regarding uniform, the length of your skirt, and you weren't allowed to eat in the street. We had conduct marks [for bad behaviour]*, and disorder marks if you did something like forgetting homework. There was a lot of rivalry and a cup awarded to the best house each year. We only had hats in winter, a green felt hat with a turn-up brim with a ribbon and badge on the front. Prior to me going, the straw boaters had been done away with. The coats and skirts were green, and a white blouse with black, white and green striped tie. In summer you wore green and white cotton dresses. They could be bought or there were Simplicity patterns that could be bought from Render's if you had a mum or relative that could make them.*

We were streamed at the end of the first year. If they thought you were reasonably good academically, you did Latin, and if they didn't think you were quite so hot, you did housecraft. I did Latin. So I can't cook, but I can swear in Latin. It's not a dead language at all, I think because of the interest in music, Latin being associated with Italian, you got the musical phrasing. We did a modern Latin course so we looked at the history as well which made it more interesting.

The fees were £68 a term when I left in 1973. Then there was the uniform, school lunches and piano lessons. If [a girl's] *father was a vicar, they got reduced fees because it belonged to the Church Schools' Company. There were scholarship girls, and it seemed to attract a lot of farmers' daughters who could afford to pay fees.*

Gillian Sowray playing bassoon on far right in Talbot room (Gillian Sowray)

It was a very happy school. We had very good teachers, traditional, quite strict, keen on being well-mannered. They treated you as ladies. You had to stand up when the teachers came in, and they always wore gowns. That was quite good fun for the music teacher, Miss Whittaker, because her room was round a corner, and she'd go at quite a fast pace and her gown would flow out behind her. Even people who didn't like music, liked her, it was the personality that she had.

There were recorder groups and choirs and we would perform at concerts for parents. Only three of us took music O level. I remember going on a recorder course to Huddersfield. I was in the same group as Miss Whittaker. There was an eminent player called Walter Bergman and he took the senior group and he was quite terrifying. I was probably 13 at the time. I played clarinet in the York schools concert at the Jack Lyons Concert Hall at the university, and one of the girls in the sixth form accompanied me on piano. I sometimes used to play the organ in St Michael le Belfry on a lunchtime. And Miss Whittaker would organise people to come in to school. David Munro and the Early Music Quartet gave an afternoon performance, and we had a chap with a harp once. Speech days were held at Tempest Anderson Hall or York Theatre Royal, with lots of musical events, entertainment and speeches.

You were treated as a more adult person, given a bit more freedom and independence. But I'm not sure that single sex schools are a good idea. You don't have the distractions but if you have boys around, it helps you to relate to them in later life. If you were a good all round person, you could get on well. If you were more interested in the arts, you found it quite limiting. I had to drop history to do music.

I had my first taste of the Great Yorkshire Show at school because they organised a bus trip in the first year. After that, you were allowed a day off to go and I went to the Yorkshire Show every year I was there.

We did country dancing at the [Minster] *Song School. I also did fencing, that was good fun. We had* [fencing champion] *Paddy Power to give us tuition. We had some excellent fencers. The school captain was the Yorkshire senior schoolgirl in fencing, Fiona Marsden. There was a girl called Lucy Ann Bleasdale in our year. She entered various competitions.*

There were two libraries, a big reference type library and one with fiction, where you got taken once a week to choose a new novel. We used [the language labs] *at King's Manor for French. We had a French lady as a teacher. We used to play up a bit. We just wouldn't listen and we'd take the mickey. She asked questions and we'd give silly answers. She retired the year before O levels and it became evident when the new teacher came in, that we knew next to nothing. She had to work hard to get people through the exams. We had a maths master called Mr Ainsworth who sang in the Minster choir so you would never get*

Interior of York College for Girls building (York Archaeological Trust)

him the last period on an afternoon because he'd have to go and sing evensong. We were quite often able to distract him to discuss relevant topics of the day. He was quite happy to do that instead of maths.

I was a music prefect in my last year, the only one that's never sung in the choir. I had to make sure that the piano and all the music were ready for assembly every morning. We'd sing a hymn, and sing a psalm to a chant and we'd have prayers and somebody would play the piano on the way out.

Looking back on our year, it was pretty mixed. Some people have done exceptionally well. Lucy Ann is an eminent lawyer in London, and we produced a lot of nurses, occupational therapists, radiographers. But there wasn't any career advice. They didn't steer us at all. Mrs Ward, the Latin teacher, moved to Queen Ethelburga's for a short period of time and then came out of teaching. She was young when she was at York College. I was at Nestlé and ended up having to interview her for a temporary job. It's a small world, too small sometimes.

Gillian feels that she didn't work hard enough at school.

I had a boyfriend from being about 14 and I was more interested in boys than studying, and out of school things rather than knuckling down and working hard. But I probably fitted in better, being in a smaller class, than I would have done in a big school. It was a very happy place.

York College for Girls building 2010 (*Christine Kyriacou*)

BOOTHAM SCHOOL

The Friends, or Quakers, have long been involved with education in York. In the 19th century they set up the city's first Adult Schools for men and women. The Mount School for Girls, came into being in 1785 and Bootham School began life as 'York Friends Boys' School' in 1823 in a house in Lawrence Street. The school had several classrooms, a library, workshop and small playground. By 1833 there were 50 boys. The site proved to be unhealthy due to its proximity to the Foss and the swampy land. One of the masters even kept a pistol handy for shooting rats. But it was an outbreak of cholera which forced the governors to move the school, and in 1846 they bought number 20 Bootham, for £4,530 and the school moved there, though it was not called Bootham School until 1889. Several other properties along Bootham were purchased over the coming years, as well as 18 Portland Street which was used as a sanatorium. The second head teacher or superintendent, John Ford, at the school from 1829 to 1865, was a keen member of the Yorkshire Philosophical Society. His interests in natural history and astronomy were to become important in the life of the school. At this time, Quakers were not allowed to take university degrees, and Ford had problems in appointing suitable teachers. Between 1866 and 1943, there were four headmasters, all of whom had been boys at the school, and then assistant masters.

Rear of Bootham School 1900s (*Image reproduced courtesy of City of York Council, Local Studies Collection*)

The Old Scholars Association was founded in 1879, and was to play a crucial role in fundraising for the school. They financed the swimming pool in 1914, and the school playing fields in Clifton, 18 ¼ acres off Rawcliffe Lane.

BOOTHAM SCHOOL

**TRAINING for
UNIVERSITY, INDUSTRY, CITIZENSHIP.**

Careful attention is given to PHYSICAL DEVELOPMENT, LEISURE HOUR WORK (Natural History, Archæology, Carpentry, etc.), EDUCATIONAL GARDENING, FIRST-AID and AMBULANCE, SWIMMING and LIFE-SAVING.

BIOLOGICAL, CHEMICAL and PHYSICAL LABORATORIES, A NATURAL HISTORY ROOM, TWO WORKSHOPS (including Forge and Metal-Work Lathe), ASTRONOMICAL OBSERVATORY, SWIMMING BATH, GYMNASIUM, HISTORY and GEOGRAPHY ROOMS, STUDIO and LIBRARY.

Full Particulars from the Headmaster,

Bootham School, York.

1930s Advert for Bootham (Mike Race)

While other public schools concentrated on classical education, Bootham has always preferred the sciences. The Natural History Society, which claims to be the oldest science society in Britain, was founded in 1834. Weekly talks by different experts were offered, such as a lecture on the sparrowhawk and the heron by old boy Ian Prest, chairman of the Royal Society for the Protection of Birds. The club held weekend excursions, and travelled to Bempton Cliffs, the North Yorkshire Moors and Conway in North Wales, as well as Askham Bog, Strensall Common and Clifton Ings closer to home.

Boys were encouraged to keep natural history diaries and to make collections of pressed plants, fossils, birds' eggs and insects. The keen ornithologists began ringing birds, of which 2000 were done in 1936. Bootham became one of the leading bird trapping stations in the country. At least seven members of the club were to be elected Fellows of the Royal Society in adult life. One, Gilbert Baker, became Curator of the Herbarium at Kew Gardens. Another member, Wilfred Alexander, produced a moth which rid Australia of the prickly pear pest.

In 1909 the society took part in the Franco-British exhibition with work done by boys out of school hours. By 1911 there were 65 boys and several masters as members. The society still thrives today and the biology department has run expeditions including a diving trip in southern

Europe and a visit to the Farne Islands and Iceland. Archaeology was also encouraged and boys assisted at excavations at Crambeck near Castle Howard, and St Mary's Abbey.

The Bootham School Observatory was installed in 1850, with two telescopes (one of which is a four inch refracting telescope made for the school in 1852 by Thomas Cooke of Cooke, Troughton and Sims), and a revolving roof, and this has recently undergone major refurbishment. Bootham's maths and physics teacher David Robinson, also a well-loved housemaster, retired in 2007, having arrived as a student teacher in 1974. He had taken over responsibility for the observatory and still conducts visits from the public. On a very starry night in early 2009, it was a privilege to join a group led by David, and to climb onto the roof and see Venus through the giant telescope.

By 1865 there were 56 boarders at the school and by the 1870s, the school had begun to admit non-Quakers. In 1882 number 49 Bootham, previously the home of Joseph Rowntree, became the headmaster's house and dormitories. Unfortunately a fire destroyed most of the schoolrooms in 1899, but they were rebuilt and reopened in 1902. Headmaster Arthur Rowntree, affectionately known as Chocolate Jumbo, supervised the work which included a new science block. The new library unveiled its plaque to John Bright, an old scholar who had become a mill-owner, Anti-Corn Law League leader, and President of the Board of Trade in 1869. In 1905 Arthur Rowntree started a summer 'lads'camp' for Bootham boys and local boys from low income families, stating that, 'We are proud to be in the tradition of promoting friendship between all classes'. He also transformed the school from an inward-looking rather closed community, to a school with a much wider range of pupils.

During the First World War, boys and masters undertook first aid training and ambulance drill. Part of the school was requisitioned for use as a hospital, and fitted out with wards and an operating theatre. In the event, they were not used, so were dismantled after only a few months. Boys from the school went to help on local farms during the summer vacation, and their wages were donated to a fund for relief workers.

The school's centenary in 1923 was celebrated in style. Funds were donated for a Centenary Bursary to assist with fees for the sons of old scholars, and to improve the sports facilities in Clifton. Joseph Rowntree donated the large house on the corner of St Mary's for the use of boarders and it became Penn House. The school has its own names for each school year. Years 7, 8 and 9 are called Lower, Middle and Upper Schoolroom. Years 10 and 11 are Lower and Upper Senior, and the sixth form consists of College 1 and 2. At one time there was also College 3, lasting for one term, for those taking Oxbridge exams.

Staff and two matrons at Bootham 1929 with Donald Gray, headmaster, centre of front row
(Bootham School Archive)

By 1928, Bootham's early distrust of competitive games had given way to enthusiasm. 'Hurdling for style' was introduced in 1933, with discus throwing and shot putting. Other leisure activities included breeding canaries, Quaker pedigrees, Hungarian music and cycling. By 1930 there were 153 pupils, which had risen to 240 in 1956. In the summer of 1936, Archbishop William Temple opened a new wing of the school. The headmaster, Donald Gray, presided over the celebrations, which began with a presentation on the master's grass of the sheep shearing scene from 'A Winter's Tale'. Polixenes was played by a young Jewish refugee from Germany, Gerhard Lackman Moss, who became a renowned historian. There was also music and morris dancing, and a display of sequence swimming in the pool.

In 1939, with the advent of the Second World War, the school moved to Ampleforth, freeing Bootham to become an extension of York County Hospital, in case of gas attacks. As in 1914, it was not needed, and the school returned in 1940. The boys were encouraged to help with ground maintenance and gardening. During the war, jazz came to Bootham under the guidance of Percy Lovell and a full swing band.

Donald Gray had become headmaster of the school in 1927. His wife Kathleen Wright had taught at the Mount junior school. He increased the school's leisure pursuits and appointed music and handicraft teachers, as well as initiating (and taking part in) productions of Gilbert and Sullivan operas. Their son David Gray was born in 1931.

My father was a pupil before the First World War. He came to the school as an assistant geography teacher in the early 1920s. I grew up at 49 Bootham, the headmaster's house, becoming a pupil from 1944 to '50.

There are three brothers, John, myself, and Roger. We were all at Bootham. Our house and the school grounds were adjacent and we saw the playground and buildings as an extension to our home. The boys were extremely tolerant, allowing us to join in games of football and cycling in the grounds. The masters were known as uncles. It was an extraordinarily warm family community. In the 1930s there was a strong tradition of bachelor resident teachers, fairly common in public schools around the country. Nowadays most teachers don't want to live on the job. When my father became head, the previous head was elderly, a bit austere and one of the old scholars said, "We just couldn't believe that Donald was going to be head because he was young and he was fun, we all liked him".

In the 1930s they looked closely at becoming a voluntary aided school, where the faith group provides the buildings and recruits the teachers but the local authority pays the salaries. In the end they withdrew that offer and we remained independent. Quaker school fees are below the average public school fees, in order to be less exclusive.

*When the Second World War broke out, my father was a close friend
of the Abbot of Ampleforth. Their junior school moved to Gilling
Castle and Bootham was invited to move into the junior house. With
the ecumenical atmosphere of Quakerism, I don't think there was
any difficulty in accepting Catholic hospitality. There is a story told
of my father addressing the two schools as, 'Friends, Romans and
countrymen'.*

*My father was in a reserved occupation. He'd worked in the Friends'
Ambulance Unit in the First World War and in 1916 served with
Naval Intelligence in Majorca. Quite a number of staff did go off to
the armed forces. Their places were taken, in part, by German Jewish
refugee teachers, because Quakers took in a lot of Jewish families at
the time of the rise of Nazis. One memory I have of my father, early
in 1939, he was very distressed because the police were coming to
intern teaching staff and senior pupils, who were carried off to the
Isle of Man.*

*One of the beliefs of Quakerism is that there is that of God in
everyone. If we live our lives rightly, we can touch that and draw
out the best in each other. People who join a Friends' school are
in sympathy with this. Quakers believe that there is no difference
between sacred and secular, and the schools teach that there is a
spiritual dimension to life. So relationships are strongly supportive
and creative, and affirmative of the best side in all of us. With the
Mount, we met regularly for drama activities and the girls would
come to Bootham to swim. We had a joint choir and we met at the
Quaker meeting house in Clifford Street on Wednesday mornings
for worship with one of the staff giving a talk. During the big air
raid in York in April '42, the school lost its sanatorium off Portland
Street. Later the headmaster's house was built there and 49 Bootham
became part of the boarding provision.*

My father died tragically in 1943 [of pneumonia] *and the Old
Scholars Association kindly helped my mother with the cost of fees
for the rest of our school days. My brother John was also headmaster
at Bootham* [1972 to the 1990s]. *When I started, my family were*

Bootham School at Ampleforth during early months of World War Two 1939 – gardening, skating, skiing (Bootham School Archive)

no longer living there but the school felt like home. For a while the school owned number 54 across the street, in which W H Auden was born. His father was Medical Officer for York.

The school never played rugby. This was one of Bootham's ways of saying it wasn't part of the general public school tradition. One of the traditions was work with children in poorer areas of York. They'd play in our gym and at football with us.

You can find bullies everywhere and they're very often unhappy children. And Bootham had its share of children from broken homes. This is one of the services that boarding schools offer when a family breaks up and sometimes the best place for a child is away from home. Bullying was the exception rather than the rule. All Quaker schools eschew corporal punishment. There's no caning and no beating and Quakers aren't keen on hierarchy.

Swimming team 1945, David Gray far right on back row (Bootham School Archive)

I loved languages, and geography, and I loved biology and remain keen on conservation, I'm a beekeeper. Physics was full of maths, I could cope with that, but chemistry seemed smelly and dangerous and I gave it up as soon as I could. I kept on trying to give up Latin but to get into Oxford, you had to do it.

Every morning the bell rang at quarter to seven, by twenty past we had to be in the library for five minutes of silence, then five minutes break before breakfast. We ate well. We had a cooked breakfast, two course lunch, a snack mid morning, a snack at four o'clock, and evening meal at 6.30. We had half an hour before lunch and were free to go into town. In the summer we had lessons after lunch and then games. In winter, games in the first part of the afternoon and lessons at 4.30 followed by prep before tea, and sometimes long prep after tea. The latest lights out were ten o'clock.

We had lessons on Saturday morning, and had Saturday and Wednesday afternoons off. We played matches with other schools, or you might get leave, for a cycle ride to Stamford Bridge or Helmsley or to some nature reserve. I often went home because I was living in Clifton. On Saturday evening we had a film or some entertainment. Sunday morning the school went to Quaker meeting for an hour, Sunday afternoon was free. Four times a term we were allowed 'flick leave' to go to the films or the theatre.

People broke the rules, that's normal. The most severe punishment was being rusticated or sent home. That happened rarely. Gating for two or three weeks was a severe punishment. We had to run round and round the playground, that was being given rounds. The main punishment was columns, you had a book of hard words to spell and you copied words in columns. The maximum was ten columns for the most serious offences. If a class acquired more than a certain amount, there was a form punishment, like detention. The sense of breaking the family relationship between pupils and staff was almost a part of the punishment. My greatest crime was to let off a firework in a Latin class taught by a dear Austrian Jewish professor. He was very good at teaching earnest graduates, not very good with small boys. I hid the firework in a metal tray underneath the radiator. It went off exactly 15 minutes after I lit the fuse. The headmaster happened to be passing by and this enormous bang shook him. He dashed into the classroom and went to all the bad boys in the back row saying, "Was it you?" And I just put my hand up. I was gated for three weeks.

Smoking was an offence with serious consequences. Of course the danger of fire was a major worry, and staff had to retire to 'the bird cage', a small attic in the head's house, if they wished to smoke.

On the whole Quakers tend to be on the left in politics. The old boy network doesn't operate in the way it can in other public schools. If you had a child that you thought might be a high-flying banker or barrister, you might go for St Peter's rather than Bootham.

Boarders with canoes and trunks 1949 (Bootham School Archive)

In the sixth form, you'd have a study with two or three other boys. But if you were a prefect you were in charge of a dormitory of younger boys, making sure there was no talking after lights out. There were seven houses. Bright, Tuke, Ford, Penn, Fox, Watson and Fryer. Names of distinguished Quakers and previous heads. We had house reading together on Sunday evenings when the house master invited us to his sitting room. We sometimes had house matches for football, cricket and swimming.

Female teachers were the exception. We had a housekeeper, and a team of women who looked after school linen and clothes, and a nurse in charge of the sanatorium. We had a marvellous maths teacher, John Stroud, he got me a distinction in mathematics, I can't imagine how. When I did my teacher training at Oxford following the degree, I asked to go and teach in Southampton where he was headmaster. This was clearly a sign of a strong affection and inspiration and he, along with a number of teachers, remain my lifelong friends. I never taught at Bootham, I did teach at other Quaker schools in Britain and America.

Bootham for me has been a family as well as a school and I can't separate out growing up as a staff child, from being a pupil, old scholar, governor, and a parent. It was a seamless web.

For the major post-war building plans, appeals had to be made for funding, and old boys were incredibly generous. New extensions and interior changes took place in 1950. The new assembly hall, designed by Trevor Dannett, was funded by appeals to old boys and parents. The library was vastly improved with new books and facilities for quiet study.

Colin Henderson attended Bootham and later returned as its bursar. He was born in London in 1931.

Colin Henderson retires as bursar 1994, with Rita Oldroyd, Clerk to the Committee (governors)
(Bootham School Archive)

The war was not an easy time for schools. The staff were all away, it was a limited curriculum. A lot of the men teachers were past retirement age and had been tempted back in, or were very young and fairly green. They had even got to the stage of having women teachers which was quite a shock, being very much a boys' school.

I went to Haberdasher's School in Cricklewood and then for the sixth form I came to Bootham in 1947. My father knew the headmaster Tom Green and his wife quite well through the Holiday Fellowship Movement, and they were Quakers.

It was fairly easy to fit in but I missed out at not having had the earlier years at the school. People had had a broader education in the lower school with things like woodwork and sport. But my fellow pupils were fine. My history teacher in particular was influential, he was able to make it interesting so he's given me a lifelong interest in history.

It was a very friendly place and relations between staff and pupils were always good. The higher you went up the school, the more you felt on a par with the younger staff.

When I came you had to learn all the words for things otherwise you didn't eat. [This was the Bootham slang]. *Milk was bull, sugar was sand, custard was quiddle, teacakes were willies, bread was bars. The prefects were called 'reeves'. I was a house reeve.*

Other examples of the slang were 'my lord' for headmaster and 'juice meeting' for telling-off. The Bootham word 'oick' for an unpopular pupil or member of another school, found its way into the Oxford Dictionary.

I think it did me good, it was a small and caring community, and the staff appeared to be there all the time. Bootham was never elegant, there were never gowns. Clothing was always fairly informal. We didn't have to wear uniform in the sixth form, apart from the blue caps with a white Maltese cross on top. We wore sports jackets and trousers.

There was always rivalry with St Peter's, mainly on a friendly basis. On November the 5th, Bootham would have a bonfire. St Peter's wouldn't because Guy Fawkes was an old scholar, so somehow we would get hold of a St Peter's cap and put it on the guy.

Bootham was good at preparing you for life after school, in terms of self-reliance. Some pupils who go to university from day schools, are almost lost and don't know how to be responsible or sensible about things. On the whole, it did rely on self-discipline. Although it was only a two year period there, it was significant and I liked the set-up and ethos enough to want to come back and contribute towards it. You do get to know people much more closely, when you're boarders. But the downside is that when you go home, the friends you made at school might live 250 miles away.

I left school in 1949, worked in a merchant bank in London for 17 years. I joined the Old Scholars and came back for reunions at the May weekend when they had a programme of activities and a dance. It's a joint thing between Bootham and the Mount still.

I decided to train as an accountant and was sent to different companies to audit their books and so I started applying for jobs as a bursar, and became bursar of the Mount in 1971.

From the 1920s, there had been a joint bursar for Bootham and the Mount, as well as a joint governing body, although they were run as separate entities. When Colin arrived, the previous bursar stayed at Bootham for five years but then,

I became bursar at Bootham also in 1976. I used to shuttle between the two. My main office was at Bootham. My office at the Mount was a cupboard under the stairs.

In the early '70s there was a move to amalgamate the two schools into one. It was impractical in the end, with the two estates, neither big enough to accommodate the whole thing. Then boarding schools throughout the country started to have a drop in numbers, particularly boys' schools. People wanted to have their children at home, the idea of sending them away for months at a time was less appealing, it was a social change. The first step was to bring in more day pupils. The headmaster, John Gray, asked for permission to take in day girls. That was not competing with the Mount because they didn't take day girls. It was quite successful and inevitably the move was broadened towards being co-educational. And then there was competition between the two schools, you couldn't run them as one organisation and the Yorkshire Quakers decided that each school must have its own governing body and bursar. So in 1991, my job at the Mount finished and I remained bursar at Bootham until I retired.

There are things I remember with great pleasure. There was a Sunday evening meeting with music, and then the house master would read a story to about 18 of us. That was the nearest we got to being a family. I didn't see my parents from the beginning of a term to the end. It was quite a long time. So to be in a community which made you feel at home was good.

The 1960s and '70s brought in much more casual dress. Boys were allowed to grow hair long, and there are photographs of masters in tank tops, flares, coloured shirts, pink ties and trendy silver glasses.

Michael and Valerie Allen met and married whilst teaching at Bootham. Michael came to the school in 1966, to teach history and English.

Quakerism was quite new to me and the North of England was even newer. But I discovered York was a clone of the south. It was a school of 250 pupils, who seemed to come as if by magic without our having to advertise and worry. The percentage of Quaker pupils, about 22 per cent, steadily dwindled. Quakers don't like private education, they believe in equality of opportunity. There is a body of opinion who believe that Quaker schools shouldn't exist but if they didn't, one of the planks of Quakerism would be removed. It's an ongoing debate.

There was far more learning by rote then. Lessons were more demanding but pupils weren't expected to take the initiatives

Michael and Valerie Allen's wedding 1980s (Bootham School Archive)

that they took later for GCSE and A level

196

projects. I always taught the history of York to the Lower School.

I was a resident member of staff. Hours were very long at times and resident staff not rewarded particularly well. But things have changed. Accommodation has improved, when it started it was quite poky. I lived on top landing, directly above the front door of number 51. I was looking after about 80 boys, boarders from 14 to 18, with the help of a matron. Any visitors had to wade through the pupils. I had my own private washbasin but shared the bathroom. I had breakfast and lunch with the school, and evening meal with staff. I was on call at nights, if somebody was taken ill I might get a knock on the door, and would ring the sanatorium. It was part of my job to get the pupils up. It was most tricky with the sixth formers.

There is a great freedom to talk, which is prized by both staff and pupils. Discipline did depend on the personality of the teacher. I think new staff did find it difficult to settle for a year or so. I didn't get much help. There were no prizes for achievement, no speech day. The thinking was that the achievements of the less able pupil were just as important as those of more able pupils. If you didn't agree with the Quaker attitude, it wasn't the right school for you. We had a number of Jews from Leeds, because we didn't try to convert. Among the staff was Alfons Wegener [he became a well-known biologist and encouraged involvement in archaeology], *who had come from Germany in the late 1930s fleeing from the Nazis. He was a lovely man, but he was interned for the duration of the war.*

All staff were expected to help with games, or to do some equivalent task. The pupils' meal was at six, there'd be a member of staff on duty and they didn't sign off until ten. I ran a chess club. I also ran the cricket which added 24 hours to my working week in the season.

In the early days the Bootham intake was not exceptionally academic. We had a reputation for getting the best out of pupils, and also for being good with pupils who had been bullied at other schools. We always had choice of what we taught. At O level I taught the 20th century, it was quite unusual, but I felt this was good knowledge for people who were going to go into a science.

In about 1967 I was sent on a course for Quaker schools about pastoral care. Each year the heads and deputies of Quaker schools meet to discuss things common to Quaker schools. At one time I used to call myself the master in charge of theft. Every so often things happen, shoplifting or whatever, and I somehow found myself dealing with this. We asked the police in once or twice to give us advice about drugs.

I was asked to be head of history and later deputy head. There has never been a female head or deputy. There were one or two women before the girls came. Ros Fitter was head of biology for a couple of years. There were music peripatetics, they weren't allowed to take morning coffee in the staffroom with the others, which was awful, particularly as one was the wife of the head of music.

With girls, the school became a cleaner place, a friendlier and much kinder place.

Education is infinitely better now, much more rounded. So many areas have had huge advances such as careers education. Standards have improved hugely. University staff have said Bootham pupils

Fox House Boys' Boarding   O

59   57   55/53

Houses of Bootham School 2010 (*Bootham School Archive*)

interview extremely well, they are used to classes where they are encouraged to contribute very freely.

Valerie Allen came to teach English and history in 1974, having taught at all girls' boarding schools.

I was quite young and a bit of a novelty. It was quite a shock, these enormous jean-clad boys with bushy hair, all much taller than me. I used to take prep on a Wednesday morning with Upper Seniors, year 11. They were very naughty, they'd chat and wander round the library and be up on the stack of books waving at me. I remember one boy, they had thick oak desks, and his mission was to bore his compass point through the lid of his desk before he left. And he used to do this all the way through the lesson. I struggled for the first year. At the end, I said, "I'm going to leave". I was living in Tockwith and they cycled out with these big bouquets of flowers and said, "We know we've been difficult, but don't leave". So I didn't.

There was very little trouble really. Drug taking in York was quite high but we were pretty rigorous. Although three little boys from Bootham raided Santa Claus's grotto in Brown's one year!

When I first started we did grammar, comprehension and précis, as well as literature. It was much more formalised teaching than it

hool Building		Rowntree House Girls' Boarding			Support Services
51		49	47	45	43/41

*later became. I used to take tea and lunch duty occasionally, prep
in the evenings. They liked all staff to do activities in the evenings,
things like drama and debating. The junior drama was all boys. They
were so funny playing girls' parts. One boy became very fond of his
tights and high heels, I was a bit worried. And we did plays with the
Mount. Every year the main production was Shakespeare or Gilbert
and Sullivan, it alternated. It was very popular, especially as it was
the only time that boys and girls got to mix much. The hall was quite
new and we had very good lighting. Initially Quakers didn't approve
of drama or plays. It was quite a bold step to do drama at all. I
did help with music. There was a joint orchestra with the Mount,
and later on house choirs. We had quite a lot of groups who would
practise when we had activity time and we had the strawberry dance
which Rowntree's ran for the sixth formers.*

Valerie became more involved when girls came to the school in 1983.

*It wasn't easy for some members of staff who felt uncomfortable
dealing with girls. They were quite confident and fitted in pretty
easily. They had their own common room for the first few years. There
were some romantic attachments, but by and large I noticed the huge
friendships between girls and boys. One girl married the boy she sat
next to on her first day there. And they've got children. It has become
increasingly flexible. There are more day pupils now. You could be
a day boarder, and stay for activities in the evening, or a weekly
boarder so you went home for the weekend. Or you could sleep in
school for a couple of nights during the week.*

*Things changed when the girls came. There was a lot of rather cruel
teasing and the girls wouldn't stand for this. They were very good
at looking after shy boys in their year groups. There'd been a thing
called 'rabble', where they would call someone a particular name or a
sound and when someone came into the room, they would make this
sound. And that went quite quickly.*

*Sex education came from the sick bay, the nurse undertook to do this.
She was very skilled. We didn't have domestic science of any sort.*

The girls did woodwork and metalwork. We used to have cooking as an evening activity. It was boys who mostly took it up. I was head of English and I was doing library and drama, and then went on senior management. It meant quite a lot of pastoral work, and keeping an eye out for the girls and making sure we weren't overlooking what they needed. It might mean dealing with romances going wrong, problems at home, bullying, difficulties with a particular person, 'Miss, I think I might be gay', almost anything. In the sixth form you had a group of six or eight students you would see through to A level, and were responsible for their pastoral and academic progress, that was quite rewarding. We did theatre trips and weekends in Stratford and London. I remember the first A level class I taught with girls, and they were looking at Othello in totally different ways and it was really good to hear both sides.

In 2007, Michael and Valerie became joint presidents of the Old Scholars Association (Valerie being the first woman in this post). They worked hard to increase the membership.

We could remember Old Scholars weekend as being exciting, you'd suddenly see these amazing sports cars and motor bikes roaring into school. And they wanted to see their old teachers. But this had dribbled away and we were asked to make contact with younger old scholars.

Today Bootham has 480 pupils. As well as the usual sports, the school offers activities such as bell ringing, croquet, juggling, board games, candle making, ceramics, hip hop dancing, water polo, fencing, horse riding and big band music. Music is an important part of the curriculum. It is departmental policy not to audition and students are encouraged to develop at their own level. The senior choir has reached the final of BBC Choir of the Year competition, and other ensembles have reached the final of the National Festival of Music for Youth.

There are many prominent old scholars. The houses display plaques to Joseph Rowntree, and Silvanus Phillips Thompson who studied and taught at the school in the late 19th century, becoming Professor of

Physics at University College, Bristol, and Principal and Professor of Electrical Engineering at Finsbury Technical College. A number of the Rowntree family members were educated at Bootham including Joshua Rowntree, the politician and social reformer, and Benjamin Seebohm Rowntree, well known as a sociologist who produced studies on poverty and unemployment in York in 1901, as well as members of other Quaker families such as the Cadburys, and the Clarks' shoe retailers.

JB (John Bowes) Morrell, a York author and historian, attended Bootham in the late 19th century. He was twice Lord Mayor of York, formed York Conservation Trust, became director of Rowntree's at the age of 25, and campaigned for a university in the city, which now has its library named after him. As a committed Quaker, he refused a knighthood.

The historian and left wing campaigner, AJP Taylor, was at the school in the 1920s and Sir Stuart Rose, pupil from 1962 to 1968, was Chief Executive of Marks and Spencer until 2009. In 1959, Phillip Noel-Baker, later Baron Noel-Baker, was awarded the Nobel Peace Prize after his campaigning for disarmament and his work for international peace. After the First World War he was heavily involved in the new League of Nations. He was an outstanding athlete and ran for Britain in the Olympic Games of 1912, 1920 and 1924, winning a silver medal in 1920 for the 1500 metres.

In more recent times, Jeremy Heywood, at the school in the 1970s, went on to Oxford and then the London School of Economics and in 1999 became Principal Private Secretary to the Prime Minister, serving under Tony Blair, Gordon Brown and now David Cameron.

The school now owns ten Georgian and Victorian houses along Bootham, numbered 41 to 59. Behind this frontage lies 'a peaceful oasis in the heart of York', with many other buildings and extensive grounds. The houses have their own individual designs with features such as Adam fireplaces, elegant staircases, ornate plasterwork decoration and sloping floors. In 2009, a beautiful Georgian ballroom was found, hidden behind partitioned walls, during restoration on the first floor of number

45. Darrell Buttery of York Civic Trust described it as 'an undiscovered sleeping princess'.

Valerie Allen feels,

We were happy there, it was a lovely place to teach, very rewarding.

Boys with trunks 1950 (Bootham School Archive)

– CHAPTER 8 –
Comprehensive Reorganisation

It is 25 years since York schools became comprehensive. Discussions about reorganisation had taken place as early as the 1950s, but it would be many years before planning could take place and before the final decision could be made.

The Yorkshire Evening Press, in the Spring of 1985, stated that Sir Keith Joseph's agreement 'ends 25 years of political wrangling and academic frustration'. The plan to close six schools, which would affect 7000 pupils, was based on the 'sixth form college principle', and the press reported that the cost involved was £6.85 million. Beckfield, Burton Stone, Derwent, Danesmead, Knavesmire, and Margaret Clitherow secondary schools closed and the Ashfield site became the Sixth Form College. Park Grove had closed in 1983, and Fulford School had already become a comprehensive. In 1985, Archbishop Holgate's, Burnholme, Canon Lee, Huntington, Joseph Rowntree, Lowfield, Manor and Queen Anne's all changed to become comprehensive schools, and Oaklands School opened where Acomb Secondary Modern had been. The Bar Grammar School became the lower site of All Saint's School, with Mill Mount becoming the upper site, and the Mill Mount girls transferred to Nunthorpe which was renamed Millthorpe.

Dr Michael Frost, the head of Archbishop Holgate's from 1978, had previously led three Midlands schools through the changeover to comprehensive education, and was appointed principal in 1983 of the Sixth Form College. An earlier head of Archbishop Holgate's, Donald Frith, believed the change to be 'a pragmatic response to a living situation, an imperfect attempt to resolve some of the anomalies, inconveniences and injustices of the previous system'.

Once the staff were appointed and the new buildings ready to open, there was excitement and expectancy for some, but for others it was a time of great tension, pain and sadness. All the closing schools held farewell celebrations, with picnics, discos and musical events. Old pupils came from near and far to the reunions, and commemorative mugs, pens or ties were purchased.

Eileen Carter, who had been teaching at Derwent Secondary Modern, describes the uncertainty of people getting posts in the schools they preferred.

Job descriptions came out and there'd be X numbers of posts for the salary scale you were on. The interview was at Park Grove, about ten or twelve of them, new heads and various people from the education department. The new head of Archbishop's, Alan Walker, moved in a year before the reorganisation. Five or six of us went there from Derwent. Quite a lot of grammar school staff went to the Sixth Form College. It did take three or four years [to settle]. You were working the grammar school out with exams and you were starting new exams and new courses and then all the changes in education.

Just about everybody got a job, whether it was the one they really wanted or not. But quite a lot of staff moved after a year or two. Some of the grammar school teachers got a bit of a shock with mixed classes and a different kind of ethos. They were in a different atmosphere completely to us who'd worked in secondary moderns with every kind of child. But with mixed schools, it was a much healthier balance.

At the end of the summer term, the Yorkshire Evening Press reported that, 'The school bell will toll for the last time today as eight of York's schools mark the end of an era. They will ring out the old selective system of education which has moulded generations of the city's children, ringing in the modern comprehensive alternative'. The York Save Our Schools Committee, described it as a 'traumatic upheaval', but supporters of comprehensive education said it was 'an exciting opportunity for York children'.

Darrell Buttery remembers discussions in the 1970s which at times had got rather heated.

Head teachers Dorothy Cook and Geoffrey Cushing discuss the merger of Mill Mount and Nunthorpe Schools 1984
(Millthorpe School)

I sat in a hall packed with teachers who had come to hear an HMI give his views on going comprehensive. It was as if we were all going to face some major operation rather than just have the nature of our schools changing.

A meeting of the Parents' Executive was followed by the annual gathering in the hall, where the head praised the school for its achievement and then in a second speech attacked the plans for comprehensive reorganisation. He claimed that the devil himself couldn't have worked out a more devastating set of plans if he had wanted to cripple the system.

Darrell recalls the last day at Nunthorpe.

For the lunch, Mr Cushing was back, and other staff who had left recently, so that it seemed more like Nunthorpe of years ago. The weather matched our feelings and Arthur Harrison summed them up when he said he felt flat. The final assembly was moving. The rendering of 'Jerusalem', loud and sad, brought assembly - and Nunthorpe - to a close.

Nunthorpe was a mixture of different classes of people in society with a very strong disciplinary code. In the comprehensive school there seemed to be so many problems that those who weren't going to work,

Last four house captains at Nunthorpe School 1985. L to R – Tim Dean (Normans), Michael Dickson (Danes), Martin Pepper (Saxons), and Andrew Lock (Celts) (Darrell Buttery)

who were going to disrupt, had more opportunity to do so. And the more sensitive, nervous bright ones, who could be bullied, shut up like clams. The staff who had stayed on from the grammar school, or come from Mill Mount were used to much stricter discipline. There were others who had very liberal ideas so there was quite a clash of cultures.

Many grammar school teachers, whatever their views, particularly missed the sixth form, where pupils and teachers seemed to have a better relationship and to feel more relaxed with each other. Darrell

desperately missed sixth form teaching. [He left Millthorpe and] *went to teach at Pocklington and I remember the strangest feeling, of actually walking on air. I was walking to my sixth form lesson, having not taught the sixth form for many years, and I couldn't feel my feet, I floated there. The rapport that you had with those sixth*

Last Assembly at Nunthorpe School July 1985 (Darrell Buttery)

formers! I told them once, because 18ᵗʰ century is my great love, an age of elegance, if I'd been born then I'd have gone round in a sedan chair. And a knock came on the staff room door next day. They had got a table, upended it and put chairs on and draped the thing with curtains, it was more of a palanquin than a sedan chair, and I was to get in and be taken to my lesson. I did miss that ability to have fun and a lot of laughter but to do work and to enjoy good results.

I've been telling people for years that I didn't like Millthorpe at all. After a while some of the children used to hum the funeral march when I went past because they could see I was unhappy, it wasn't my sort of school. There was a lot of clan rivalry and behaviour which I'd never seen before. But in theory I think I accept comprehensives.

Richard Nihill is the only man to be a pupil at Nunthorpe Grammar School and Millthorpe Comprehensive and a teacher at Archbishop Holgate's.

I was the last academic year to take the 11 plus. Nunthorpe was running along the lines of an old fashioned grammar school, partly dictated by the staff and partly by the history of the buildings. My first year was boys only, in the second year the Mill Mount girls came and joined us. We were ultimately a grammar school cohort, and then Knavesmire closed and the secondary modern pupils came.

We were mixed up in terms of form groups with a mixture of ex-grammar school and secondary modern. I think the grammar school system served me well and when it became comprehensive, I benefited from the good bits of the comprehensive system and of the secondary modern system. It's not always easy for one institution to serve the needs of pupils with such a broad range of ability.

I do recall some very challenging pupils. I remember we were watching videos on the Second World War, and when the teacher left the room, they fast-forwarded the video, and I remember a boy climbing out of the window. I wonder whether some of the ex-grammar school staff, though very academically able, were used to teaching pupils who were desirous to learn, and therefore perhaps didn't have the skills to discipline difficult pupils.

With Archbishop Holgate's, I get the impression that when it went comprehensive, it went through a difficult period. It could be argued that when York went comprehensive, did the senior leadership and the director of education, actually facilitate teaching in a comprehensive? It's different to teaching grammar or secondary modern. I wonder

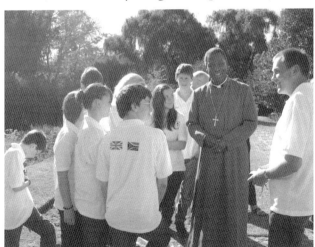

Richard Nihill and his class from Archbishop Holgate's in Cape Town meet Archbishop Thabo (Richard Nihill)

whether some staff were almost left to flounder. It's very easy to blame the pupil or the staff but maybe they were just left to struggle.

The way our education system works, to succeed in education you have to be able to sit exams and write essays. I don't agree that mixed ability is the best way forward. I think teaching in sets helps everybody. Where the teachers can know the pupils, where the head can know the pupils, where communication is relatively easy and there is a sense of a school identity, those are really valuable things. Having specialisms is a good idea. Now you see teachers sharing expertise with other schools, and sharing skills, sometimes sharing resources and facilities. That is something to encourage. As a teacher at Archbishop Holgate's but also a staff governor, you're aware of management issues and demands that come from government and of the severe financial constraints that all schools are working under. There is limited money in education. League tables and Ofsted grades lead to competition. It does put schools under pressure. You've got to

Archbishop Holgate's School 1992. Eileen Carter is fourth from left on front row. Head teacher John Harris is in centre on front row (Eileen Carter)

strike the balance between aspiring and encouraging.

My schooling gave me the ability to value education. I enjoyed my school days, I made good friends, I think I learnt some good values. At the start of every term, Dorothy Cook would read the part from Corinthians about there being many parts to the one body, and explain that as a school, there are many parts and we should value one another.

The 20th century saw huge changes in secondary education, in York's schools as in the rest of the country. There will continue to be changes in the future, with the advent of 'academies' and possibly 'free schools' run by parents. The input from parents today, with open days, parent-teacher associations and parent governors, is a long way from the Victorian schoolroom where education was nothing to do with parents and a matter for the teachers alone.

The period of schooling, whether happy or not, is a crucial stage in a child's life. Their future career, as well as their relationships with others, may well be determined by how they are treated and how well they 'fit in'. Jonathan Taylor, the head of Bootham, says, 'We asked parents what they thought should happen in a classroom…their suggestions tallied with the teachers'experience : a tolerance of different viewpoints, a genuine interest in an individual's contribution, a sense of support and sharing, and a recognition of equality of worth…The pressures exerted on us which must regulate, monitor, and inspect are pressures towards uniformity. Maintaining an element of individualism becomes increasingly important'.

An advertisement for an independent school outside York, asks -

"What makes a good school?
First class dedicated teachers, a caring environment, good facilities, and an ethos that every child has a role to play in school life.
What makes a great school?
All of the above and the knowledge that whatever a child's strengths, they will be recognised, nurtured and enhanced".

This may seem idealistic, but perhaps all schools should strive for this child-centred education. The experiences of those featured in this book show that what happens at school has an enormous effect on the rest of a person's life, and that it is important to both challenge and nurture a child, and seek out each one's particular skills and talents.

The Archbishop of York, Dr Michael Ramsey, in a speech at Archbishop Holgate's Grammar School in 1960 said that, on his move to York, "I came to realise that it is the people of a city, whether old or new, who constitute it, and make it what it is. And among the people of a city, it is its schools which really constitute it. Those schools train their young people, and fashion their character over the years to come. Its schools are the lifeblood of the city".

Glossary Of Secondary Schools In York

ACOMB COUNTY SECONDARY MODERN SCHOOL
Opened in September 1954. The senior department of Acomb Board School in Front Street was transferred there. Had 470 children in 1956. Extended in 1978 but closed in 1984 and the school became Oaklands.

APPLEFIELDS SCHOOL
School in Bad Bargain Lane for secondary children 11-19 with special educational needs. Opened 2004 with 135 pupils.

ARCHBISHOP HOLGATE'S SCHOOL
Founded in 1546. 140 boys attending in 1899. Given direct grant until 1944, by 1949 it functioned as independent school but became voluntary aided secondary grammar school for boarding and day pupils. Became comprehensive school in 1985.

ASHFIELD SECONDARY MODERN SCHOOL
Opened on Tadcaster Road, Easter 1957, incorporating boys from Scarcroft Secondary School. Girls joined later that year. Closed 1985 and site became Sixth Form College.

THE BAR CONVENT
Set up in 1686 as a boarding school by the Institute of the Blessed Virgin Mary, first Catholic institute for teaching girls in the country. The day school opened 1699. Became direct grant school in 1929. Damaged in 1942 air raid when some of the nuns were killed. After the Second World War, accommodation doubled by adding seven classrooms, laboratory, needlework room and dining room. Became known as the Bar Grammar in 1977 and began to admit boys. Became lower school of All Saints Comprehensive in 1985.

BECKFIELD SECONDARY MODERN SCHOOL
Opened in Beckfield Lane in 1948, the first of new secondary moderns to open in the city after the war, it replaced the senior department of Poppleton Road which had been transferred to Scarcroft School in 1942. 560 pupils by 1956. Closed in 1985 and demolished for housing in 1986.

BLUE COAT AND GREY COAT SCHOOLS
Blue Coat School for Boys was based at St Anthony's Hall, Aldwark, from 1705, and the Grey Coat School for Girls was in Marygate from 1705, moving to Monkgate 1784. Founded for poor children, often orphans, who attended until 13 or 14 and were prepared for apprenticeships or domestic service. By 1818 they each had 52 children. The Blue Coat produced many stalwarts of the city including some Lord Mayors. But ill-treatment and severe punishments were often said to be unacceptable. In 1929, the Grey Coat girls moved to Blue Coat School which closed in 1946.

BOOTHAM SCHOOL
Founded in Lawrence Street as Friends' School and moved to Bootham in 1846. Moved to Ampleforth for a few months at start of Second World War. Well-known for Natural History Society and Observatory. Strong involvement with the Mount School, originally having joint bursar and joint governors. Although originally majority were boarders, now mostly day pupils. Admitted girls in 1983.

BURNHOLME COMMUNITY COLLEGE
Opened as Burnholme County Secondary Modern in Bad Bargain Lane in 1948. Senior department of Tang Hall School transferred there. Had 560 pupils in 1956. Became comprehensive in 1985. Now a specialist Business and Enterprise College.

BURTON STONE LANE COUNTY SECONDARY MODERN SCHOOL
Constructed from 1939 and opened October 1942 in Evelyn Crescent on Water Lane estate, it was originally known as Water Lane Modern Secondary School for Girls. Accommodation for 320 girls but only 104

enrolled in 1943. In 1947 the girls from Park Grove were transferred there. School was extended in 1945. 560 girls there in 1956, and when it closed in 1985 most girls transferred to Queen Anne's.

CANON LEE SECONDARY MODERN SCHOOL
Built in 1941 and named after Canon A R Lee, chair of governors, to serve the Clifton and Rawcliffe area. Became comprehensive in 1985. Councillors voted to merge with Queen Anne's in 1997 but this was overturned by the Education Minister in 1998. The school was praised by Ofsted in 2000 and the Lord Mayor opened £4.5 million extension in June 2001. In 2005, it gained Specialist Schools status as an Arts College.

CASTLEGATE HIGHER GRADE SCHOOL
Opened 1890 for girls and infants and was staffed by sisters of the church. Fees 9d for girls and 6d for infants. In 1897 there were 107 children. Closed July 1905, reopening in September 1905 as the independent St Margaret's Girls' School, which moved to 54 Micklegate. Higher Grade school in 1920s and 1930s. Demolished in 1969, and in 1984 a copper beech was planted on the site (near to Fenwick's).

DANESMEAD SECONDARY MODERN SCHOOL
Opened in Fulford in 1954, replacing senior department of Fishergate. 480 pupils in 1956. It closed in August 1985, part of the site in Fulford Cross became the York Steiner School.

DERWENT SECONDARY MODERN SCHOOL
Opened 1959. Featured on BBC programme in 1965, extension built in 1969. Celebrated its Silver Jubilee 1983, closed 1985 and most of pupils transferred to Archbishop Holgate's.

ELMFIELD COLLEGE
Primitive Methodist school founded 1864, prominent in 1920s as boarding school, owned and managed by its old boys. Buildings, in grounds of 30 acres, included laboratory, gym, workshop, steam laundry and sanatorium. Milk, eggs and vegetables came from the college farm. Closed 1932 and united with Ashville College in Harrogate.

FISHERGATE SCHOOL
Opened in 1895 for seniors, juniors and infants. 700 senior children were there in 1932. In 1945, the Senior Department was renamed Fishergate Secondary Modern School, and was on the upper floor of school, but moved in1954 to Danesmead.

FULFORD COUNTY SECONDARY SCHOOL
Built in fields to the south of Heslington Lane in 1956 but the owner broke off negotiations. It finally opened in 1964. Transferred from East Riding to York. Seen as a country school, with many children coming from outside villages. In 1970 a swimming pool opened. Announced it would become comprehensive in 1970, York's first school to do so. New senior school to stand alongside the old school was built 1972. Stephen Venables, who taught there in the 1980s, was the first man to climb Everest (in 1988) without oxygen and is now one of the country's most respected expeditionists. Now a Mathematics and Computing College.

FULFORD CROSS SPECIAL SCHOOL
Built on site of Fulford Open-Air School at a cost of £62,704, housing the children with learning difficulties from Fulford Field House, opening in 1965. Closed in 2004 and became Danesgate Pupil Support Centre.

FULFORD OPEN AIR SCHOOL
York's first open-air school opened in Castlegate in 1913, but it was not satisfactory and land was bought by the council beside Fulford Field House in 1914 to house a school for special needs children, and an open-air school for those with physical ailments such as TB. The First World War intervened and the War Office needed the buildings for military use so the schools did not open until 1919. The open-air regime was a new concept and became very successful. The front part of the building had sliding doors to open the school to the air. Children were taken from pre-school age up to 14, but once cured, the children were moved to other schools. Closed by 1960, and children transferred to Northfield Special School. Demolished in 1964.

HAUGHTON'S SCHOOL
Founded 1770 by benefactor William Haughton, to educate 20 children in parish of St Crux, this number increased and by 1864 there were 34 boys. Moved from Fossgate in 1901 to St Saviourgate. Later became an independent school. Fees were three guineas for day children, and 20 guineas for boarders. Closed in 1956.

HUNTINGTON COMPREHENSIVE SCHOOL
Opened in 1966, became comprehensive in 1973. Awarded £232,000 government grant in 1992 to develop as a Design and Technology College. Now has a sixth form and 1500 pupils, in 2009 was the only state school in York to offer the International Baccalaureate Diploma.

JOSEPH ROWNTREE SCHOOL
Originally secondary modern school, opened in 1942 in New Earswick, then in the North Riding, not the city of York. Initially tended to provide more practical subjects such as rural studies and motor vehicle studies. Became comprehensive in 1985 and specialist Technology College in 1998. In March 2010 it moved into a £29 million state of the art building and won an award as the Most Versatile Learning Environment. Its eco friendly features include rainwater harvesting, biomass boiler, use of natural sunlight and ventilation and a weather station.

KNAVESMIRE SECONDARY MODERN SCHOOL
Knavesmire Council School opened in April 1916 on Campleshon Road, and became one of York's higher grade schools. In 1945, with the new tripartite system, it split into a primary school and a secondary modern school for girls. It moved to Middlethorpe in 1964 and admitted boys in 1965. Closed 1985 and became the College of Law in 1988.

LIME TREE HOUSE SCHOOL
Private school, situated in Monkgate, the principal in the 1930s was Miss Ingleby and the school advertised, 'Highly qualified staff of English, French and music mistresses, with special advantages for music and art... individual attention to 'backward or delicate' pupils. Boarding and day school for girls and kindergarten'.

LOWFIELD SECONDARY MODERN SCHOOL

Opened in Dijon Avenue, Acomb, in 1960. Half the boys from Ashfield Secondary Modern transferred there. Became comprehensive in 1985, and Oaklands school came to merge with it in 2003 to form York High School until the new school was built for 1000 pupils in Cornlands Road. Closed 2007, several arson attacks made it necessary to demolish it in 2010.

MANOR SCHOOL

Opened in 1812 to promote the education of poor boys at Merchant Taylor's Hall, moving in 1835 to King's Manor. The building was requisitioned by the war department in 1915 and the school moved to Haxby Road. In 1922 it purchased the old York Industrial School in Marygate. Was hit in the 1942 York air raid, and moved temporarily to Priory Street. Having been a boys' school, it merged with Priory Street school in 1947 to become mixed. Moved to Low Poppleton Lane in 1965 and became comprehensive in 1985. Moved again in 1999 to Millfield Lane, Poppleton. The new school cost £18 million, and is now a specialist Performing Arts College.

MILL MOUNT GIRLS GRAMMAR SCHOOL

The house, in Mill Mount Lane, off the Mount, was built in 1850 by JB and W Atkinson and opened as Mill Mount Secondary School for Girls in 1920. In 1926 fees were £4.4s a term. Accommodation for 381 pupils. It became a grammar school and fees were abolished, in 1944, and in 1985 it closed, with the girls transferring to the old Nunthorpe School, to become Millthorpe Comprehensive School.

THE MOUNT INDEPENDENT SCHOOL FOR GIRLS

Founded as a boarding school in Trinity Lane in 1785, then housed in Castlegate. In 1857, moved to its present site in Dalton Terrace. Combines a co-educational junior department with a girls' senior school with a Quaker ethos and is the last single sex secondary school in York.

NORTHFIELD SCHOOL

Originally opened in 1965 on Beckfield Lane as Northfield Open Air School for children aged 5 to 16 with physical and other disabilities. (See Fulford Open Air School). Closed 2004.

NUNTHORPE BOYS GRAMMAR SCHOOL

Built as a fine Victorian house in 1856, and used as a hospital in the First World War, it became a secondary school for boys in 1920, with 49 boys, a 'brother school' to Mill Mount. In 1944, it became a grammar school and fees were abolished. In 1985 it merged with Mill Mount to become Millthorpe Comprehensive, with pupils from other schools joining in 1986. It has no sixth form, pupils transfer to the Sixth Form College.

OAKLANDS COMPREHENSIVE SCHOOL

Opened in 1984 in premises of Acomb Secondary Modern School. Opened first Dyslexic Unit in 1998. Later took over the sports centre next door on Cornlands Road. It moved to Dijon Avenue to merge with Lowfield to form York High School and in 2007 returned to a new school on the original site in Cornlands Road. Now York High School, a Specialist Sports College.

PARK GROVE SECONDARY MODERN BOYS SCHOOL

Park Grove Board School opened 1895 and in 1899 the lower standards moved to Brook Street. In 1932 there were senior, junior and infant departments. The girls were transferred to Water Lane Girls' School, later Burton Stone School, and the school became boys only. It closed in 1983.

POPPLETON ROAD SECONDARY SCHOOL

Mentioned in York Education Committee minutes, when in 1946 they were advertising for head teacher, and Mr Kneebone, master at Nunthorpe, was appointed. Badly damaged in the 1942 air raid, and pupils attended Scarcroft School. After the war it became a junior school.

PRIORY STREET HIGHER GRADE SCHOOL
A school for boys, girls and infants was built next to Wesley Chapel in 1857 and opened 1858, under Methodist management. In 1857 there were 373 boys, 130 girls and 214 infants. By 1894 it had places for 848. It was first described as higher grade school in 1897. Extended in 1905 with an Arts and Crafts building in front of part of the school and new block opened 1911. Reorganised by 1932 to senior department and junior and infants. In 1936 only the seniors were left. Boys from Manor merged with it in 1947, and it closed in 1948, pupils going to the new Manor School.

QUEEN ANNE'S COUNTY GRAMMAR SCHOOL FOR GIRLS
Pupil teacher centre opened in Brook Street School in 1905, it was officially recognised as secondary school in 1908. The boy pupil teachers were accommodated at Archbishop Holgate's. 210 girls were enrolled in 1908. The Brook Street premises closed 1909 and girls transferred to the new building at the bottom of Queen Anne's Road, Clifton, the first secondary school to be built as a school, with accommodation for 270 girls. New classrooms erected in 1914, 465 girls were there in 1946. Became comprehensive in 1985 and closed in 2000.

ST DENYS' SENIOR SCHOOL
Situated in Dennis Street, Piccadilly for children up to 14. After the Second World War it became a junior school only.

ST GEORGE'S SECONDARY MODERN FOR BOYS
St George's Junior School opened a separate higher grade department in 1928, but in 1936 a new boys' secondary school was built on land in George Street off Walmgate. The school officially opened in 1948. It closed in the 1970s and was demolished in 1996, making way for flats.

ST MARGARET'S CHURCH OF ENGLAND SCHOOL
Private school founded 1905 in Castlegate and later moved to 54 Micklegate. It had 188 girls aged 5 to 17, and ten boys under 8. It closed in 1968.

ST MARGARET CLITHEROW GIRLS SECONDARY MODERN (ORIGINALLY BLESSED MARGARET CLITHEROW SCHOOL FOR GIRLS)

The managers of St Wilfrid's School bought land in 1938 in Bad Bargain Lane but the Margaret Clitherow School (replacing senior girls of St Wilfrid's) did not open until 1963. It closed in the 1980s and pupils went to All Saints' Comprehensive School. Vandals caused fire damage to the empty school in 1987 and the building was taken over by St Aelred's Primary School.

ST PETER'S SCHOOL

Considered to be Britain's oldest public school, built 627 AD. It takes pupils from 13 to 18, many having attended the prep school, St Olave's. Originally primarily a boarding school, it now takes boarding and day pupils. The Old Peterite Association was founded in 1886. The school had 65 boys in 1900. The distinguished scholar Alcuin was first a pupil then headmaster. The teaching seems to have been divided into two sides, classical and modern, one for the clergy and one for laity. The school took its first girls in 1976 in the sixth form, not becoming fully co-educational until 1987. It also took over Queen Anne's School in 2001.

ST WILFRID'S SECONDARY MODERN SCHOOL

Catholic School in Monkgate, completed in 1875. In 1910 there were two departments, mixed and infants. A new block was built to be the higher grade school in 1928. In 1938 there were 159 in this department and 293 in the junior and infants. The managers were going to build a senior department in Monkgate but instead bought land in Bad Bargain Lane in 1938 for £1600. Secondary girls were being housed in the Rectory of St Maurice, Monkgate. In 1963, the new Blessed Margaret Clitherow Secondary School for Girls (later St Margaret Clitherow) opened in Tang Hall and St Wilfrid's remained a junior school.

SCARCROFT SECONDARY MODERN SCHOOL FOR BOYS
Opened 1896, the fourth York Board School, built by Walter Brierley. Reorganised into senior, junior and infant departments. In 1950 it had a championship swimming team. In 1956 there were 280 boys. Recognised by English Heritage as 'an example of the best of Victorian educational architecture'. The boys moved to Ashfield School in 1957 and it became a primary school only. Its language laboratory was used by other schools in the 1960s.

SHIPTON STREET SCHOOL
Shipton Street Board School was opened in 1891 with accommodation for 660, the first school erected by York's new school board. There were 440 children attending in 1892. In 1910 there were 288 enrolled in the boys' dept, 278 in the girls', and 202 in the infants. In 1912 the boys' department was closed and transferred to Brook Street School (see Park Grove). In 1942 the senior girls' department was transferred to the new Water Lane School; in the same year the school was slightly damaged by enemy action. In 1956 there were 580 in the junior school and 180 in the infants'. It closed in the 1980s and remains boarded up, awaiting conversion to flats.

TANG HALL COUNCIL SENIOR SCHOOL
Situated in Sixth Avenue on the Tang Hall estate, for pupils up to 14. After the Second World War, it became a junior school only.

YORK COLLEGE FOR GIRLS
York Church High School for Girls was founded in 1891 in Minster Yard and moved in 1908 to Petergate to become York College for Girls, an independent day school. From 1919 there was accommodation for 30 boarders at Burton Grange in Clifton but this had closed by the 1930s. After a prolonged battle by staff, pupils and parents, the school closed its doors in 1997, with 234 pupils moving elsewhere.

YORK HIGH SCHOOL
York's newest secondary school is a Specialist Sports College with currently 1000 pupils. It replaced Lowfield and Oaklands Schools, and opened in 2009 at a cost of £13 million.

THE YORK MODEL SCHOOL/
ST JOHN'S VOLUNTARY AIDED SECONDARY MODERN SCHOOL
Opened in 1859 as a demonstration school for the York and Ripon Diocesan Training College in Lord Mayor's Walk, (later St John's College). In 1899 they were combined in a new building with accommodation for 338 boys. Fees were 7s 6d a quarter. French, Latin and shorthand were extra. Designated an elementary school in 1900 and in 1932 it became a boys' secondary school, and after 1948 continued as St John's Voluntary Aided Secondary Modern school for boys, with 200 pupils in 1956. It closed in 1965.

YORK SIXTH FORM COLLEGE
Opened 1985 on site of Ashfield Secondary Modern, utilising part of the old school. It merged with York College of Further and Higher Education in 1999 to become York College, both campuses finally amalgamating to become the new York College at Sim Balk Lane in 2007.

YORK STEINER SCHOOL
Developed by Rudolf Steiner in Austria, the York school opened in Bishophill in 1981 and later moved to Fulford Cross on the site of Danesmead. It has 200 pupils aged 3 to 14. It is organised around the philosophy that children 'find joy in learning and are not pressured by tests'. Maths and the alphabet are not taught until the age of six.

YORKSHIRE SCHOOL FOR THE BLIND
Was based at King's Manor, for adults and children, from 1833, sharing the building with the Manor School. It closed 1956 and pupils transferred to other cities.

Bibliography

BARKER, Ray (Ed.) *The Last Windmill. Mill Mount Grammar School for Girls.*
Mill Mount School, 1985

BENSON, *Edwin. History of Education in York 1780-1902.*
Unpublished Phd thesis. York University, 1932

BROWN, Sidney. *Bootham School 1823-1973.*
Sessions, 1973

BUTTERY, Darrell. *Nunthorpe Grammar School 1920-1985.*
Nunthorpe Grammar School, 1985

BUTTERY, Darrell. *Extracts from Diaries 1970s and 1980s.*
Unpublished.

DRONFIELD, J. *'Education' in The Noble City of York*
(Ed. Alberic Stacpoole). Cerialis Press, 1972

EVANS, Geoffrey. *A History of Manor C.E. School 1812-1994.*
Manor School, 1994

HUNTER, Geoffrey (Ed.) *Archbishop Holgate's School, York. 1546-1996.*
Archbishop Holgate's School, 1996

JEWELS, Ernest. *The History of Archbishop Holgate's Grammar School 1546-1946.*
Westminster Press Printing Group, 1946

KNIGHT, C. B. *A History of the City of York.*
Herald Printing Works, 1944

LLOYD, Jean. *The Story of a School, Brook Street to Queen Anne 1910-1985.*
Queen Anne's School, 1985

MORRIS, Bridget, Robinson, David and Smith, Barry. *Natural History at Bootham – the Early Years.*
Sessions Book Trust, 2009

TILLOT, P.M. (Ed.) *Victoria History of Counties of England. A History of Yorkshire: City of York.*
Institute of Historical Research, Oxford University Press, 1961

Kelly's Street Directories

The Mitre. Magazine of Archbishop Holgate's Grammar School
The Nunthorpian. Magazine of Nunthorpe Grammar School
The Sphinx. Magazine of Queen Anne's Grammar School
The Windmill. Magazine of Mill Mount Grammar School
Derwent Secondary School magazine 1983

Official Guide to Civic Week York 1934
Official Guide to York 1929-30, 1934
York City Council Education Committee Minutes. 1940s, 1970s, 1980s.
York City Yearbook 1931.
Yorkshire Evening Press

Publications by the Same Author

The History of a Community: Fulford Road District of York.
University College of Ripon and York St John 1984, reprinted 1985

Alexina: A Woman in Wartime York.
Voyager Publications, 1995

Rich in all but Money: Life in Hungate 1900-1938.
York Archaeological Trust, 1996. Reprinted 1997. New edition 2007

Beyond the Postern Gate: A History of Fishergate and Fulford Road.
York Archaeological Trust, 1996

Humour, Heartache and Hope: Life in Walmgate.
York Archaeological Trust, 1996

York Memories.
Tempus Publishing, 1998

Number 26: The History of 26 St Saviourgate, York.
Voyager Publications, 1999

Voices of St Paul's: An Oral History of St Paul's, Holgate (Edited).
William Sessions, 2001

Rhythm and Romance: An Oral History of Popular Music in York. Volume 1 : The Dance Band Years.
York Oral History Society, 2002

Something in the Air: An Oral History of Popular Music in York. Volume 2 : The Beat Goes On.
York Oral History Society, 2002

Rhythm and Romance: CD of The York Dance Band Era.
York Oral History Society, 2003

The Walmgate Story.
Voyager Publications, 2006. Reprinted 2009

Something in the Air: CD of York Music in 1960s.
York Oral History Society, 2006

Rations, Raids and Romance : York in the Second World War.
York Archaeological Trust, 2008

Stonegate Voices.
York Archaeological Trust, 2009

The Story of Terry's.
York Oral History Society, 2009